AMERICA LOOKS

A Pamphlet S

No. 12

THE UNITED NATIONS ECONOMIC AND SOCIAL COUNCIL

By

DR. HERMAN FINER

London School of Economics and Political Science,
University of London, England, and now
Visiting Lecturer on Government,
Harvard University

1 9 1 4 2

WORLD PEACE FOUNDATION

BOSTON

1946

WORLD PEACE FOUNDATION

40 Mt. Vernon Street, Boston, Massachusetts

Founded in 1910

THE World Peace Foundation is a non-profit organization which was founded in 1910 by Edwin Ginn, the educational publisher, for the purpose of promoting peace, justice and good-will among nations. For many years the Foundation has sought to increase public understanding of international problems by an objective presentation of the facts of international relations. This purpose is accomplished principally through its publications and by the maintenance of a Reference Service which furnishes on request information on current international problems. Recently increased attention has been focused on American foreign relations by study groups organized for the consideration of actual problems of policy.

CONTENTS

THE UNITED NATIONS
ECONOMIC AND SOCIAL COUNCIL

CHAPTER I

WORLD ECONOMIC AND SOCIAL
INTERDEPENDENCE

THE international conferences of recent years make it manifest that we are entering the age of highly and deliberately concerted international economic and social interdependence. Not that there is, or as yet can be, any tenable suggestion of a superstate or a federation of nations, even of regional dimensions. But there is a movement toward a unified effort in the development and use of the resources and wealth of the whole world. The evidence for this emerges from the international conferences on such specific institutions of cooperation as the Food and Agriculture Organization, the International Monetary Fund, the International Bank for Reconstruction and Development, the Civil Aviation Organization, the International Labor Organization, as well as from certain declarations made by the governments of individual nations regarding reconstruction, full employment, anti-depression policy, tariff reductions, colonial development and export policy in relation to employment and social security. Moreover, the Philadelphia Conference of the International Labor Organization [1] of May 1944 widened the scope of that Organization's responsibilities, with the purpose of giving it a continuing concern for stabilizing and raising the productivity of the world's economic system.

We are therefore in the presence of three related phenomena. First, there is a more intelligent and tenacious recognition of the importance of international economic and social

---

[1] Hereafter referred to by its initials I.L.O.

development. Secondly, new world agencies of economic and social cooperation are arising; there is an expansion in the scope of authority of existing ones, and there are now in existence others like the Economic and Financial and Health Organizations of the League of Nations which will be reorganized in some form. Thirdly, the United Nations Charter specifies that a purpose of the United Nations is "to achieve international cooperation in solving international problems of an economic, social, cultural, or humanitarian character," while the Preamble itself recites the determination "to promote social progress and better standards of life in larger freedom," and "to employ international machinery for the promotion of the economic and social advancement of all peoples."

Certain questions arising out of these three factors need the most searching discussion. For they will be very much with us in the next decade. Progress toward long-term prosperity in an undeveloped world order will need swift attention. The surest basis for steady and successful evolution of world economic and social policy, in its two chief forms, reconciliation of the policies initiated by individual countries and common plans formulated by the various duly authorized world agencies, lies in the public's appreciation of the benefits and difficulties of such a process. It is intended to pursue the analysis on this level. At the outset two emphatic observations must be made. It is not the object of this paper to advocate a world economic policy, or economic policies for individual countries. It is intended, however, to adopt the approximate consensus of the most authoritative students and the findings of official public bodies as the standard of international purpose. And, as has been suggested, any notion of a superstate or a world plan is firmly rejected. We explore a world task and a world opportunity, in which for the most part the coordination of national economic policies will be a happy maximum attainable at this stage of international relations.

It is not surprising that the Charter of the United Nations includes important recommendations regarding economic and social activities. Long before the Dumbarton Oaks Conference statesmen and officials of the League of Nations, of special bodies like the I.L.O., individual government spokesmen and delegates to international conferences recognized that a coordinating "roof" organization would be essential to contain and guide all special international economic bodies. Stimulating such recommendations was the experience of the League of Nations. The Covenant [1] included in a less specific form, indeed, and certainly with less consciousness and assurance than the Dumbarton Oaks Proposals and the Charter some provisions for promotion of international economic advancement. In the earliest drafts of the Covenant, American and British statesmen concentrated their attention entirely on security. But very soon two things were realized. First, security and peace itself might be assisted or threatened by the economic situation of the world. Secondly, the spectacle of a shattered and disintegrated world economy caused by World War I, and the deep impression made by the revelation of the immense technical, scientific and organizational skill that went into its prosecution, strongly suggested that here was opportunity to make a contribution to an almost universally higher standard of living, if only the proper organization were furnished.

This is most evident in the contribution of Field Marshal Jan Christiaan Smuts in his pamphlet, *The League of Nations— A Practical Suggestion*. Characteristic passages, which were of great effect on the Covenant, may well be cited at this stage of peace-making and reconstruction following World War II:

"Not only a possible means for preventing future wars, but much more a great organ of the ordinarily peaceful life of civilization, the

[1] In Article 23; and in the Preamble's phrase "In order to promote international cooperation."

11

foundation of an international system will be erected on the ruins of this war. . . . It is not sufficient for the League merely to be a sort of *Deus ex machina* called in in very great emergencies when the spectre of war appears; if it is to last, it must be much more. It must become part and parcel of a common international life of states, it must be an ever visible, living, working organ of the policy of civilization. It must function so strongly in the ordinary peaceful intercourse of states that it becomes irresistible in their disputes; its peaceful activity must be the foundation and guarantee of its war power. . . .

"Quite recently the practice of the Allies in controlling and rationing food, shipping, coal, munitions, etc., for common purposes through the machinery of Allied councils has led to the idea that in the future a League of Nations might be similarly used for the common economic needs of nations belonging to the League—at any rate for the control of articles of food or raw material or transport in respect of which there will be a shortage. In other words the economic functions of the League will not be confined to the prevention of wars or the punishment of an unauthorized belligerent, but will be extended to the domain of ordinary peaceful intercourse between the members of the League.

"Questions of industry, trade, finance, labor, transit and communication, and many others, are bursting through the national bounds and are clamoring for international solution. Water-tight compartments and partition walls between the nations and the continents have been knocked through and the new situation calls for world government. If the League of Nations refuses to function, some other machinery will have to be created to deal with the new problems, which transcend all national limits. The task is there; all that is required is a carefully thought out form of government by which that task could be undertaken."

He also suggested that the League should be charged with the establishment of equality of trade conditions by removing economic barriers between its members and assuring free transit by land, water and air.

Such ideas eventuated in Article 23 of the Covenant, particularly Section (e). In the interwar years a very substantial contribution was made to world economic and social development by the League. From this first stage of this world

12

experiment many lessons have been drawn. The stipulations of the United Nations Charter then are not without ancestry. They are the result of sober perception that a high degree of economic interdependence already links the nations of the world.

CONTROLLING IDEAS

It is most essential to comprehend the economic and political thought underlying the proposals for specific world economic and social agencies—"the specialized agencies" as the Charter names them—and for a world roof organization over them all. This leads us back to some elementary but controlling ideas.

1. *Economic Welfare and War*

It is difficult, in general, to affirm a relationship between economic welfare and war, such, for example, as that a country suffering unemployment and destitution and with a low standard of living will be tempted to make war, or that economic competition among nations will drive them into conflict. It might be possible to show that some contribution to warlike attitudes is made by economic distress in specific wars, but it would still be impossible altogether to single out the economic from the psychological and spiritual causes which make for outbreaks. Even if this could be done, to attribute to the economic factor a decisive influence would be impossible in any war in modern history. But it might be said that where people are economically destitute, they may become politically desperate, and therefore be prepared to follow fanatical and misguided leaders, who may then lead them to war. Also, there is a long-range remote heaping-up of rivalries for markets and raw materials, but these are irritants, not causes. And the era of colonial wars is over or about to close. However, since humanity must anticipate all risks, there is at the minimum a prudent argument for economic cooperation to raise the stand-

13

ard of living and offer all peoples economic hope and opportunity as an offset to the lure of war. The addition to each country's wealth of a proportion of what it might get by hazardous foreign adventures for *Lebensraum,* may be by so much a reduction of any stimulus to extend their boundaries. We can at least make sure of that.

2. *The World's Loss from Poverty*

There is, however, a more enduring reason than avoiding war for encouraging world economic and social government. It is the dreadful poverty of by far the larger part of the world, living much below the minimum level of nutrition warranted in modern scientific judgment. In view of the unpopularity of the role of international Santa Claus, and even in some Christian lands, of the Good Samaritan, no policy of charity to others is suggested. Appeal is made to a hard-headed policy of self-interest. The physically destitute are bad customers of the few great industrial nations. Their economic feebleness weakens the welfare of the economically advanced countries themselves. As soon as a subsistence level is overtaken, there is a very high elasticity of demand for many of the so-called tertiary goods (manufactured and highly processed by skilled workers) made by the advanced nations. Policies of full employment together with a rising standard of living cannot be fulfilled in the advanced nations at present unless the backward nations' power to consume and pay for that consumption is increased. We return to this theme again presently. But all policies of economic prosperity for poor as for rich countries ought to begin with Mr. Colin Clark's summary: [1]

"Summarizing these figures, the world is found to be a wretchedly poor place. An average real income per worker of 500 International Units or less (in round figures a standard of living below two pounds

[1] Clark, Colin, *The Conditions of Economic Progress,* N. Y. and London, Macmillan, 1940, p. 2, 3.

or $10 per week per breadwinner) is the lot of 81 per cent of the world's population. A standard of living of 1000 International Units per worker per year or more is found only in the U. S. A., Canada, Australia, New Zealand, Argentina, Great Britain and Switzerland, containing between them 10 per cent of the world's population. Another 9 per cent of the world's population is found in the principal industrial countries of Europe with an average real income per head between 500 and 1000 International Units. About 53 per cent of the world's population, including the whole populations of India and China, enjoys a real income per head of less than 200 International Units. Average real income per breadwinner in China and India is about 120 and 200 International Units respectively."

The hundreds of millions who thus barely live cannot possibly be customers for the typical products of the industrial countries, whether articles of consumption or the great variety of light and heavy machinery or tools of production on the land and in the factories that might enable them to increase their own productivity, and so permit them to save and acquire capital to attain economic self-help. These industrial countries also lose the benefit of low prices for their own consumers arising out of lower cost of mass production.

3. *Distribution of Population and Industry*

Another important consideration must be added. The development and location of population and industry as the world pattern is today was not controlled by a unified principle. The economic pattern of the world is not chaotic, but it is rational only in the sense that individual and national activity was deliberate. It was at no time concerted by all for the superior common ends of all. It is the difference between a plan after world-thinking, and the fortuitous product of various egoisms of limited vision. Over several centuries, but particularly the last two, a long series of larger or smaller business and financial engagements were made by individuals or firms in manufacture, commerce, agriculture, shipping and finance, and were supplemented by treaties of commerce and other

15

such international instruments and national management and protection.

The initiative came chiefly from Northwestern Europe, with the U. S. A. as a later and mighty factor, and the economic course taken was in their primary interest whatever the incidental benefits to the rest of the world. The way was opened for the international distribution and exchange of the various products of the different nations and thus for the exploitation through the so-called international division of labor of the advantages of each. The process, though not without purpose and good sense, was piecemeal. However, it gave the already wealthy and powerful the advantage of accidental priority.

4. *Distribution of Raw Materials and Industry*

Similarly, there was no previously planned relationship between the concentration of populations and industry and the location of certain important raw materials. For example, the population and the manufacturing and agricultural needs of the United States up to the end of the nineteenth century developed in entire disregard of the part which tin, rubber, tungsten, chrome, among other things, would come to play in the lives of the American people. And so also with other advanced countries, in relation to a great variety of commodities mined or grown under national sovereignties far from the centers of the industrial users. The new needs and inventions of the richer one-third of the world's millions were developed without regard to the location of necessary raw materials. Development therefore proceeded on the assumption that no obstacles to imports would arise, and stable means of payment would be available.

The national economies based on overseas supplies and markets set the pattern for the lands upon which they depended. The controlling power had no special interest in the economic development of the masses in these areas. These masses found their occupations, standard of living, the size of the population

16

and its education, to a large extent affected by the economic purposes of the outside world over which they had no control.

5. *Dependence of the National Economy on the Network of Trade*

There is yet another vital fact. The internal economic structure of each separate country is a response to confidence in its position as part of the network of international trade and specialization of production. The growth of wealth in each land has depended to a considerable extent upon reliance on imports and exports. This has affected the distribution of the people in various occupations, and contributed, often decisively, to the size of the national income, and even to the educational arrangements necessary for recruiting the workers by hand and brain needed in the different types of industry. Today, for example, the British educational system is undergoing drastic reform partly as a preparation to meet future export necessities. There is a direct relationship between the educational system postulated in the "Bombay Plan for the Economic Development of India," [1] the size of the population, the expected foreign credits and technical assistance, and the goods upon the production of which an increase in per capita wealth depends.

That the balance of each country's economy is separable from that of all others only at a disastrous cost and abrupt readaptation of all, may be seen, for example, from the relative positions of Germany and Great Britain as regards the number of workers required in each country to feed one thousand of its population. The different balance of the occupations of each country for this purpose will be noted. It will be appreciated that these differences are related to home resources and foreign trade, the different fertility of the land, the types of skill which must in each be cultivated, and the population and

[1] See "The Bombay Plan" by P. S. Lokanathan, *Foreign Affairs,* vol. 23 (July 1945), p. 680–7.

its standard of living. To feed 1000 consumers the following workers are required: [1]

	GREAT BRITAIN	GERMANY
Working on the land	24	96
Making agricultural machinery, materials, etc.	10	14
Making exports to pay for imports of food and feeding-stuffs	21	4
Distributing and manufacturing foodstuffs	43	48
Total	98	162

6. *"Foreign" Trade a Misnomer*

It is thus of fundamental importance to recognize that to talk of "foreign" trade is to be entirely out of date. The more "foreign" trade becomes important to us, the less we can talk of "foreign" trade. There is no such thing as "foreign trade." The meaning of this paradox leads to a consideration most essential to the object of this paper.

It has already been demonstrated that the pattern of today's world economic structure is the product of an adjustment of interests by individuals, firms and countries slowly and gradually developed over centuries. The essence of this plan (if we understand that the plan is the product and not a point of departure) is that each country has established on confidence in its permanence an economy which assumes the continuation of all the factors which support the arrangements it regards as of greatest advantage to it. So the standard of living, the occupations, even the size of the population all taken together as a concerted system in each country, are not the product of isolated economic units, but of an extensive and profound interdependence.

In order to emphasize not only the lesson of interdepend-

[1] Cf. Crowther, Geoffrey, *Ways and Means of War*, N. Y., Oxford University Press, 1940, p. 42.

ence, but a peculiar imperative relationship of domestic policy and international economic collaboration, reference may be made to the social security system proposed by Sir William Beveridge.[1] This standard of domestic national welfare heavily depends for its fulfillment upon British exports, which determine the level of employment and wage rates and labor standards. There is also an ineluctable connection with education, housing and nutrition. World War II has immensely strengthened the tendencies of social policy which were incubated during the world-wide depression. Each country has a policy of full employment and a rising standard of living, together with a very considerable increase in the social services of education, nutrition, housing, medical service, leisure enjoyment and reduction of hours, as well as comprehensive schemes of social insurance, that is income-maintenance during unemployment and distress. All this becomes a charge on the national budget which itself is nourished by national income from work and investment. All nations adopting these policies will look for internal stability of the factors of production which build up the national income. If there is domestic change, it is to be hoped that it will be in the direction of a scaling up of benefits. If there is change, as there must be to keep pace with invention, changing demand, the rise of new industries and the decline of others, then it must be controlled change, if social commitments are to be met. Most of all, an anti-depression policy will be essential. But we have amply seen that all national economies are dovetailed. No economy can break itself loose from established expectations without breaking itself, as it is a part of a whole to which each part contributes. This new factor, new, not because there was no social policy in individual countries in the nineteenth and early twentieth centuries, but because of the highly organized form it takes and the resolute temper of the masses, makes more acute the need for international economic collaboration.

[1] *Full Employment in a Free Society*, N. Y., Norton, 1945, 429 p.

Corresponding to the conditions of economic interdependence expounded above, various official bodies have recently formulated objectives of policy. An excellent summary postulated by the Delegation on Economic Depressions of the League of Nations may well be cited: [1]

"We believe that the objectives of economic policy should be to assure:

1) that the fullest possible use is made of the resources of production, human and material, of the skill and enterprise of the individual, of available scientific discoveries and inventions so as to attain and maintain in all countries a stable economy and rising standard of living;

2) that, in so far as possible, no man or woman able and willing to work should be unable to obtain employment for periods of time longer than is needed to transfer from one occupation to another or, when necessary, to acquire a new skill;

3) that in the use of these productive resources, the provision of goods and service to meet the essential physiological needs of all classes of the population in food, clothing, house room and medical care, is a prime consideration;

4) that society distribute, as far as possible, the risk to the individual resulting from interruption or reduction of earning power;

5) that the liberty of each individual to choose his own occupation is respected and is promoted by equal educational opportunities;

6) that the liberty of each country to share in the markets of the world and thus to obtain access to the raw materials and manufactured goods bought and sold on those markets is promoted by the progressive removal of obstructions to trade;

7) that the benefits of modern methods of production are made available to all peoples, both by the progressive removal of obstructions to trade and by courageous international measures to reconstruction and development."

If it is desired to maintain and improve the beneficent and even indispensable complex of international economic and social relationships these aims must be pursued with understanding and the proper machinery.

[1] *The Transition from War to Peace Economy*. Report of the Delegation on Economic Depressions, Part I, p. 14 (League of Nations Publications 1943. II. A. 3). N. Y., Columbia University Press, Agents.

CHAPTER II

WORLD ECONOMIC PURPOSES AND WORLD AGENCIES

FUNCTIONAL PROBLEMS TO BE SOLVED

Reserving until later the detailed examination of the provisions of the Charter of the United Nations for the economic and social functions of the General Assembly and the Economic and Social Council, it may be said at this stage, that the Charter provides world economic and social objectives and methods of attaining them. The objectives are the attainment of conditions of stability and well-being, the promotion of higher standards of living, full employment, and conditions of economic and social progress and development, and the solution of international economic, social, health and related problems. The principal method is the coordination of the policies and activities of the specialized agencies in the field of international economic and social affairs. The opportunities thus opened, and the conditions of their successful use, can be appreciated only by an exploration of the functional problems to be solved.

A program of international economic cooperation should strive to aim at producing the maximum amount of goods at the lowest cost, and reducing mankind's toil while raising the standard of living. This means a world economy without the national or regional boundaries that hamper the free and harmonious specialization of productive activities among producers all over the world. It requires the free movement of all who wish to migrate, the free movement of goods for consumption, the unhindered movement of raw materials and semi-manufactured and manufactured goods for use in production, the free circulation of capital for economic development and the unfettered transmission of skills and science, including patents. In order to minimize work (and it is *not* an economic ideal to have all people fully employed at a low standard of living, but vice versa) and raise the standard of living, another and deliberate policy of expansion by directed economic investment is required.

Incalculable wealth is lost to the world as a result of certain national obstacles and international private economic arrangements. These obstructions indicate the future activity of the Economic and Social Council, its Commissions, the Assembly and the Secretariat. These agencies must knit together the economic initiative of the various national units, it being understood that already some unity has emerged from the spontaneous arrangements which have been made between individuals and firms living in different countries, often assisted by treaties between their respective states.[1]

Certain tasks of interweaving and coordination stand out conspicuously. They are:

1. Freeing the channels of commerce by (a) the reduction of tariff barriers, and (b) the avoidance of excessive and unexpected fluctuations in foreign exchange.

2. Opening opportunities for the migration of peoples as one way of relieving existing maldistribution.

3. Developing the economies of backward areas.

4. Assuring equality of access to raw materials.

5. Improving labor and social standards in different countries.

6. Controlling in the general interest international commodity agreements and cartels.

7. Establishing adequate international regulation of aviation, shipping and telecommunications.

---

[1] McClure, Wallace, *World Prosperity as Sought Through the Economic Work of the League of Nations*, N. Y., Macmillan, 1933; cf. Ridgeway, George L., *Merchants of Peace*, N. Y., Columbia University Press, 1938.

8. Improving the production and distribution of food in the interest of better diets for the people of the world.

9. Taking necessary measures to protect and improve the health of people throughout the world.

10. Creating better understanding among peoples of each other's ways of life and special problems, so as to provide a sound basis for international cooperation.

For each of these functions of world economy an agency or organization of world-wide scope could be established with advantage. It would be possible to break down these various sectors into divisions and sections. But what scheme will ultimately be most advisable depends on conditions existing from time to time. Much may be learned from the experience both of the governmental development within the separate states and from the evolution of the Technical Organizations of the League of Nations.

EXISTING AGENCIES

Let us consider some of the agencies that exist and some that clearly ought to be established—the relationship between the agencies themselves, and with the Economic and Social Council and the Assembly.

The following world agencies exist at the present time or are in the process of being established:

(a) The International Labor Organization.

(b) The League of Nations Economic and Financial Organization, the Health Organization of the League, the Communications and Transit Organization, the Intellectual Cooperation Organization, together with the various committees, commissions,[1] and the Secretariat.

---

[1] (1) Permanent Advisory Commission for Military, Naval and Air Questions, (2) Permanent Mandates Commission, (3) Commission for Enquiry for European Union, (4) Advisory Committee on Social Questions, (5) (a) Advisory Committee on Traffic in Opium and Other Dangerous Drugs, (b) Permanent Central Opium Board, (c) Supervisory Body, (6) Supervisory Commission, (7) Committee on the Allocation of Expenses, (8) Advisory Committee of Experts on Slavery.

(c) Food and Agriculture Organization of the United Nations.

(d) The International Monetary Fund and the International Bank for Reconstruction and Development.

(e) The International Civil Aviation Organization.

It is customary to include among world agencies the United Nations Relief and Rehabilitation Administration. Since we are concerned with long-term considerations, it is perhaps better to omit it except to say that since UNRRA's work may last rather longer than was anticipated, especially regarding displaced persons, agricultural production and restarting the basic utilities, its work ought to be linked with that of the Food and Agriculture Organization.

AGENCIES NOT YET ESTABLISHED

If it were seriously intended to deal with the problems listed above, it would be necessary to add to the organizations that already exist: (1) a World Migration Organization; (2) a World Commission on Commodity Agreements and Cartels; (3) a World Commission on Communications and Transit into which eventually the Civil Aviation Organization might fit, but which either now or in the future would include shipping, railways and perhaps electricity in certain great regions of the world; (4) a World Trade Authority; and (5) an Educational and Cultural Organization of the United Nations.

ANALYSIS OF FUNCTIONS OF SPECIALIZED AGENCIES

Now the main purpose of this study, it must be recalled, is not to advocate or even to expound the objects and constitution of each of these agencies, but by analyzing their functions, to reveal the necessity and nature of their cooperation and so to discover the proper role of the Economic and Social Council. It is advisable to analyze the general functions which international bodies not yet established might be called upon to assume, and therefore also, their connections with other agencies.

24

No attempt can possibly be made to reproduce in any detail in the text the constitution of each of the specialized world economic agencies.[1] Attention must be centered on the purposes and general scope of authority of certain of these agencies and first, since it is the oldest, of the International Labor Organization.

THE INTERNATIONAL LABOR ORGANIZATION

It is concerned, characteristically, not so much with the increase of production, or the provision of work, or changes in the organization of industry for productive purposes, as with attaining social justice in the distribution of such products as the existing economic system happens to provide. Such subjects as hours of work, regulation of the labor supply, a living wage, protection of the worker against sickness, disease and injury, provision for old age, and freedom of association are part of its program. From time to time the I.L.O. has memorialized the League organizations or world economic conferences regarding anti-depression policy. In 1931, it attempted to secure international coordination of the public works policies of the separate nations in order to avert the economic clashes resulting from separate action.

It was recognized, however, that the work of the I.L.O. as defined above was seriously handicapped so long as it could not deal with conditions of production. There was the great paradox that the I.L.O. had authority to promote advanced standards of working conditions inside the factory, but no power to plan international measures which might make sure that there would be jobs. Consequently, stimulated especially by the demands of workers who have a constitutional voice in the organization, the I.L.O. in May 1944 decided on an increase in the scope of its responsibilities by means of "A Dec-

[1] Relevant excerpts are to be found in the pamphlet entitled *The United Nations in the Making: Basic Documents,* published by World Peace Foundation, Boston, 1945, 130 p.

laration Concerning the Aims and Purposes of the I.L.O.," known as "The Philadelphia Charter."[1]

Some of the problems with which the I.L.O. has been concerned will be briefly analyzed and the relationship of the work of the I.L.O. to that of other international bodies in dealing with these problems will be suggested.

1. *Labor Standards*

The I.L.O. has responsibility for the improvement of labor standards, that is to say, for reducing hours of work, raising wages, improving managerial and labor relationships, developing conditions of health and safety within the factory, establishing rest periods, holidays, etc. Whether such labor standards can be established or not depends upon two things: the relative strength and good will of labor and capital where the wealth of a country is substantial enough to allow for a margin one way or the other, and more important, the size of the national income.

Labor standards depend upon the prosperity of industry. If that prosperity is high, labor standards can be high. The General Assembly and the Economic and Social Council would, in seeking to achieve such prosperity, count on the investment and loan policy of the World Bank, and private banks and investors might be encouraged by the vigor and good sense of the action of the Bank. Such investments might affect not only the prosperity of the individual borrowing countries but that of nations in trading relations with them. Furthermore, the labor standards of countries in which investments and loans are made will depend, in part and more directly, on the conditions of the loans. One of the conditions of a loan is the length of time required for its repayment. This raises the question of taking out of current consumption the fiscal means necessary for meeting repayment. For example, if any considerable attempt were made to assist Chinese agriculture and

[1] For text see *ibid.*, p. 102.

26

industry, very large sums of money would be involved.[1] But the problem of countries such as China is precisely that they must reduce consumption and labor standards, in order to save capital (which is practically impossible and certainly most painful) or to borrow (which is usually the only feasible way). There ought then to be a permanent working relationship, of some kind, between the World Bank which is giving the credits and the I.L.O. which is interested in labor standards. It is the duty of the I.L.O. to see that the standards of all countries in the world advance with proper coordination.[2]

2. *Migration of Workers*

The I.L.O. was compelled to concern itself with problems of migration for two reasons. The problem of labor standards immediately arises where workers migrate for permanent settlement or a transient work period. They may need protection, or the workers in the country they enter may need protection from them, if they should bring with them a readiness to accept lower labor standards than their hosts. Before the war, the I.L.O. adopted specific recommendations toward meeting this situation. In a world as unsettled as ours will be in the aftermath of World War II (even when the main tasks of UNRRA are accomplished), migration will be an even more serious concern. Some countries which have suffered war devastation will seek to keep their workers from migrating, at least for the period necessary to set in train the main reconstruction and beginnings of normal production. Some may

[1] China—a government program of moderate industrialization would require a total capital outlay of one billion U. S. dollars expendable in a period of five years, one-half to be raised in China and the other half abroad. But this would be extremely moderate compared with the needs, and in fact meager. See Fong, H. D., *The Industrialization of China*, National Planning Association Pamphlets, Nos. 12–13, p. 80.

[2] For a practical illustration, see I.L.O. *Official Bulletin*, XXVI (December 1, 1944), p. 185–91, where the U. S. proposals for a World Bank and Fund are the subject of correspondence between the I.L.O. and the United States Secretary of Labor.

receive workers from ex-enemy countries to restore their destroyed regions. There will be the problem of opening lands to immigrants.

Experience shows that where a region is in a stage of intensive development, problems of enlisting both capital and labor and, in the economically backward countries, of recruiting technicians and skilled workers arise. Suppose, for example, that it were desired to develop the rubber resources of the Amazon Valley. Suppose it were found too expensive to cut roads through the great forests and provide railway communications. This might very well involve the provision of loans for airports, planes, housing and equipment, health services, the provision of water and other community utilities. At the same time, to ensure the success of the venture, a special search for skilled workers and technicians to teach and organize the work of Brazilians might be needed, not only in Brazil, but in other countries.

This single hypothetical case affords a vivid insight into the need of cooperation between two organizations, namely, the World Bank and the I.L.O. Moreover, analogous situations might involve the assistance of a third world agency. There are other areas, for example in China, or in India, where the raising of the standard of living is directly dependent upon a practical plan of irrigation, the provision of better seed, the provision of or erection of fertilizer plants, improvement in the agricultural skills of the cultivators and, perhaps, the migration from an area of some of the people already in it. And in addition there might well be need to improve communications, as, for example, the making of roads and the linking-up of villages, and even the provision of buffalo carts with pneumatic tires. The scheme would require the cooperation (if the matter were taken seriously at a high stage of supervision and assistance) of the Food and Agriculture Organization, a Migration Office, if there were one, and the Bank of Reconstruction and Development which would facilitate the loans necessary for the works mentioned, and perhaps, in addition, hydroelectric power, storehouses, refrigeration plants, processing warehouses and fertilizer factories.

3. *Full Employment*

The necessary interaction of the various world organizations is especially obvious and important for full employment. Full employment in each country at a high level of income is the standard of action embodied in the Declaration on the Aims and Purposes of the I.L.O. of 1944; and more, it is an objective of the United Nations Organization. Now it is inconceivable that full employment will be realized, together with the highest standard of living available at our present-day scales of organization and technology, without the maximum possible world division and specialization of production followed by the unhampered exchange of the resultant products. This implies the reduction if not abolition of tariff duties. It may be that soon a world tariff authority [1] will be set up to achieve agreement among the nations of the world on the lowering of their tariffs. If this is not done, it is certain that the Economic and Social Council and the General Assembly of the United Nations Organization must take this up. In any case, the International Labor Organization's interest in full employment implies a special collaboration with any such body. Indeed, at the International Labor Conference of May 1944 there were not wanting voices—Australia's strongest of all—which regarded full employment as a more important object of policy than anything else. The Australian Government proposed, unsuccessfully, the establishment of a special world body; [2] but eventually at San Francisco secured its aim in the form of Article 55.[3] Also, there was inserted in Article 56 [3] the pledge of joint and several fulfillment by Members of obligations

[1] Cf. p. 46 below.
[2] *International Labour Conference, 26th Session, Philadelphia, 1944, Report of Proceedings*. Montreal, International Labour Office, 1944, p. 29, 312.
[3] Cf. p. 117 below.

which they assumed in respect to economic and social co-operation.

4. Public Works

The policy of national public works to supplement employment when private enterprise fails led, during the great depression, to the establishment by the I.L.O. of an International Public Works Committee whose function it was to promote uniformity of action and to obviate the damage some countries' financial expedients caused to others.[1] At least three world authorities have an interest in the public works policies of all the member states. The World Fund would be interested from the point of view of the effect of such programs on the value of the national currency of its members. Secondly, the World Bank for Reconstruction and Development would be concerned if called upon to provide loans for such public works. Its object is the general normal expansionist development of economies rather than their partial salvaging by public works during times of emergency, but there are points where anti-depression measures and development policy converge. Finally, the provision of full employment would be affected by international cartel arrangements (private production agreements) and international commodity agreements (governmentally arranged or promoted production and purchasing agreements) which establish prices and quotas of production. The action of a cartel may directly affect the standard of living, that is the wages, employment and other conditions of work, of masses of individuals far away from the center of decision.

5. *Workers' Health*

The I.L.O. has for many years been concerned with workers' health. This has two sides to it, the environmental factors like workshop conditions, and secondly, the personal services like medical assistance and nutrition. But such responsibilities are

[1] *The Transition from War to Peace Economy,* cited above, p. 62–5.

30

necessarily interwoven with those of some of the other international organizations. For example, development schemes fostered by the Bank for Reconstruction and Development in backward areas would involve the establishment of health services, even if only for the very narrow object of securing the working efficiency of labor. The Bank, eager for repayment, might lay down conditions of economic profitability so strict that the health of the workers was a secondary and almost neglected consideration. It is at this point that the long experience of the I.L.O. (cooperating, if epidemics were involved, with the future equivalent of the League of Nations Health Organization) could play a useful role. The exploitation of the Bolivian tin miners should give pause to all those who believe that economic development by international means ought to proceed without the collaboration of a welfare agency.[1] In fact, the U. S. Government attempted to insert into the contracts with the Bolivian mine owners, in return for the high wartime prices it paid, better labor conditions for these miserable creatures. The Brazilian Government at San Francisco pressed for the immediate implementation of the health functions of the Organization, calling attention to appalling epidemics brought by airplane from Africa.

The relationship between working capacity and diet is now, thanks to the researches of experimental physiologists, and the development of the economic consequences of these studies by the League of Nations Mixed Committee on the Problem of Nutrition [2] clearly established. Firm public policies are capable of being formulated in clear statutory terms. But this implies a connection between the specialized agency concerned

[1] *Labour Problems in Bolivia. Report of the Joint Bolivian-United States Labour Commission.* Montreal, International Labour Office, 1943.

[2] Orr, Sir John Boyd, "The Role of Food in Post-war Reconstruction," *International Labour Review*, XLVII (March 1943), p. 279. See also *Final Report on the Relation of Nutrition to Health, Agriculture and Economic Policy* (League of Nations Publications 1937. II A. 10) and *Workers' Nutrition and Social Policy*, Geneva, 1936, I.L.O. Studies and Reports, Series B, No. 23.

with labor welfare and the Food and Agriculture Organization whose principal purposes are, among others:

"Raising levels of nutrition and standards of living of the peoples under their respective jurisdictions,
Securing improvements in the agencies of production and distribution of all food and agricultural products,
Bettering the condition of rural populations,
And thus contributing toward an expanding world economy."

6. *The Welfare of Colonial Peoples*

The Covenant of the League imposed a special responsibility for the welfare of colonial peoples so far as mandated areas were concerned upon the mandatories, and at the same time established an obligation on Members of the League to care for the terms of the trusteeship. The main burdens were borne by the Permanent Mandates Commission of the League, and, by virtue of its own independent authority to secure social justice for labor, by the I.L.O. To secure the obvious advantages of collaboration, the I.L.O. was given membership on the Mandates Commission. Through the device of annual reports by the mandatories to the Commission, which then reported to the Council of the League, the fact of trusteeship for the dependent peoples was made a progressive reality, even if the progress registered was not perfect. The presence of a majority of experienced colonial officials on the Commission, and the contribution of the expert knowledge of the I.L.O. produced considerable reforms, in all colonies, not merely mandated areas. Even more important than this, was the steady and cumulative mobilization of world opinion that the principle of trusteeship should be further developed and be applicable not only to mandated but to all dependent areas. For its part the I.L.O. was able to secure the acceptance of four important conventions regarding forced labor, the recruiting of indigenous workers, contracts of employment and penal sanctions,[1] and in May 1944 secured the establishment

[1] Cf. *Social Policy in Dependent Territories*, Montreal, International Labour Office, 1944. Studies and Reports, Series B, No. 38.

of a veritable charter of social policy in dependent territories.[1] One of the lessons of earlier experience was the dependence of colonial development on world prosperity.[2]

There can be no doubt, I think, that experience of mandates administration under the League, and the ripening of international public opinion regarding the fate of colonial peoples, stimulated by discussions like those so often brought into the open by the League and the I.L.O., helped to engender the sections of the United Nations Charter on "Non-self-governing Territories," and "the International Trusteeship System." There is bound to be a close interweaving of the work of the Health Organization, the Migration Authority, the International Bank, and the I.L.O. with the Trusteeship Council set forth in the Charter, which acts under authority of the General Assembly. The Declaration applies to all non-self-governing territories whether put under the Trusteeship Council or not. It makes provision for the application of certain principles of economic policy as well as other matters, and these are closely linked with all other strands of policy in the various spheres of the specialized agencies. If the work of the Trusteeship Council should go beyond mere supervision and report, actually to the direct administration of areas in trust of the Organization itself, then the work of the specialized agencies would come into contact with the execution of policy by the Trusteeship Council. At this point it is only necessary to signal that such principles have been established, and that a Council is provided for, so that the inclusion of all the specialized agencies in a network of principle and a coordinated system of action may be appreciated.

The Food and Agriculture Organization

The purpose of the Food and Agriculture Organization has already been stated in general. Its many functions may be

[1] International Labour Conference, 26th Session, 1944, *Record of Proceedings*, p. 585–602.
[2] Cf. *Social Policy*, etc., cited above, p. 15.

seen in its Constitution, relevant parts of which are reproduced in *The United Nations in the Making: Basic Documents,* referred to above. Examination of some of these functions emphasizes the importance of the continuous cooperation of the F.A.O. with other international organizations. Some instances will make this clear. The F.A.O. is to collect, analyze, interpret and disseminate information on nutrition, food and agriculture. We have already suggested the connection with the work of the I.L.O. as regards problems of nutrition. The Statistical Division of the I.L.O. has made investigations of the diet of most of the countries of the world. Furthermore, the Permanent Court of International Justice declared that the I.L.O.'s jurisdiction included not merely industrial labor but agricultural.[1] The question arises, then, whether the I.L.O. will continue with its responsibility for this aspect of the welfare of agricultural labor, or whether this should be undertaken by the F.A.O. There is much to be said for the claims of each Organization. The I.L.O. approaches the subject substantially from the angle of the all-round interests of agricultural workers; the F.A.O. from the standpoint of a new and better pattern of production and diet throughout the world. Cooperation must be devised, so that both the workers' welfare as well as the policy of scientific production on the basis of a world nutrition policy shall be furthered. Furthermore, the welfare of agricultural laborers may be affected by policies requiring that some of the agricultural population shall turn from agricultural to part-time or full-time industrial work.[2] This is clearly a matter for the I.L.O. yet within the sphere of interest of the F.A.O. For the former, the connection between the welfare of the industrial workers, and the agricultural workers, by

[1] Advisory Opinions, Nos. 2 and 3, August 12, 1922. The difficulty of severing economic factors from each other may be noticed in the Court's Third Advisory Opinion, which attempts to sever "means of production" so far as they benefit the workers and "organizing and developing production from the economic point of view."
[2] Basch, Antonin, *The Danube Basin and the German Economic Sphere,* N. Y., Columbia University Press, 1943.

reason, perhaps, of a sudden or steady shift of the latter into industrial employment, is a serious problem. It is for reasons of this kind that the I.L.O. foresaw the need to scrutinize the policies and measures of national and international agencies, so that at the proper time it might offer its comments and make its recommendations.

Let us consider in more detail some of the functions of F.A.O. as stated in Article I of its Constitution.[1] "The conservation of natural resources," which usually comprises land reclamation, irrigation, defenses against soil erosion, soil recovery, a scientific forestry policy, requires large financial resources. This involves credits, and this involves an appeal to the Bank. Moreover, the adoption of improved methods of agricultural production requires, among other things, better ploughing, planting and harvesting, perhaps even power-driven, agricultural machines. Again credits are required and this, too, may mean an appeal to the Bank. It might be noticed that one-third of all America's production of agricultural machinery has been sold abroad, that is to say about one-third of America's employment in the agricultural machinery industry is for the world market. The connection between this function of the F.A.O. and full employment is plain. Furthermore, the adoption of improved methods may involve cooperative action by farmers and tenants. In the fostering of cooperatives the I.L.O. has taken a leading role.[2]

The improvement of processing, marketing and distribution of agricultural products must mean among other things, especially for the backward countries, the establishment of warehouses, silos, refrigerators, especially constructed ships and barges, chemical plants and railways, trucks and factories, perhaps driven by electrical power for canning and dehydrating.

[1] *First Report to the Governments of the United Nations by the Interim Commission on Food and Agriculture,* Washington, August 1, 1944, Appendix I, Constitution, p. 41.
[2] Cf. *Cooperative Organizations and Post-War Relief,* Montreal, International Labour Office, 1944, Studies and Reports, Series H. No. 4.

The processing and storage saves from spoilage, or saves for a better market some distance off, or for some time in the future, a product which is available locally but cannot be consumed before it rots or can be used for exchange with products of other areas which have their own surpluses. The plans of the Chilean Development Corporation, now in its sixth year, and assisted by credits from the U. S. Export-Import Bank, are based largely on such agricultural storage and processing improvements.[1] This itself is an economic service of the very first order, not only preserving products from waste and encouraging production, but smoothing out prices over time and area.[2]

All this requires much capital, and for backward economies, credit. The World Bank's responsibilities are clear. But some organization is needed which might facilitate the recruitment of skilled workers and technologists already familiar and practiced in the processes to be adopted. The services rendered by U. S. officials on missions to the South American countries and to China are examples to be followed on an international scale.

It is already clear that this implies what the Constitution of the Food and Agriculture Organization goes on to say, namely "the adoption of policies for the provision of adequate agricultural credit, international as well as national." If the F.A.O. does not establish a credit fund, which it has not done but might do, it would have to look elsewhere for funds, and the most natural place would be the World Bank. And should the World Bank be more concerned with industrialization, then there might be added to it a special agricultural division with an increase in the total guarantee fund at the disposal of the

---

[1] For the Chilean Development Corporation, see *International Labour Review*, L (November 1944), p. 635.

[2] Finer, Herman, *The T.V.A.: Lessons for International Application*, I.L.O., 1944, Studies and Reports, Series B, No. 37, especially Chapters XI and XIV; and Hall, N. F., *Preliminary Investigation into Measures of a National or International Character for Raising the Standard of Living* (League of Nations Publication 1938. II. B. 4), N. Y., Columbia University Press, Agents, p. 7.

Bank. In any case there would be agricultural advisers, and there should be a liaison with the F.A.O.

Finally, the Organization is to seek "the adoption of international policies with respect to agricultural commodity arrangements." This subject was one to which the Interim Commission gave much anxious attention, but since it merges with the wider problem of international commodity agreements and the control of cartels, we discuss this at a later stage.

Now, the Food and Agriculture Interim Commission, which was established by the United Nations Conference held in May 1943 at Hot Springs, Virginia, for the purpose of preparing a plan for a permanent organization in the field of food and agriculture, had the great advantage of advice on the drafting of the Constitution of the F.A.O. from those with experience in already existing world organizations, and at a time when the problem of the interrelationship of the part and the whole had come into the forefront of discussion among the agencies themselves and in the schemes made by various post-war reconstruction groups. The Interim Commission wisely accepted Article XII entitled "Cooperation with Other Organizations," the terms of which read:

"1. In order to provide for close cooperation between the Organization and other public international organizations with related responsibilities, the Conference may, subject to other provisions of Article XIII, enter into agreements with the competent authorities of such organization defining the distribution of responsibilities and methods of cooperation.

"2. The Director-General may, subject to any decisions of the Conference enter into agreements with other public international organizations for the maintenance of common services, for common arrangements in regard to recruitment, training, conditions of the service, and other related matters, and for interchanges of staff."

The objective and the particular phraseology deserve the highest commendation; but the Constitution goes even further. Article XIII lays down the general relationship of the Organization "to any general world organization." This says: "(1)

37

the Organization shall in accordance with the procedure provided for in the following program constitute a part of any general international organization to which may be entrusted the coordination of the activities of international organizations with specialized responsibilities." Here is an acknowledgment of the importance of collaboration under the authority of such an organization as the Economic and Social Council of the U.N.O. Then, Paragraph 2 of Article XIII, lays down the need for ratification by the Conference of arrangements for defining the foregoing relationship, and requires that no such arrangements shall modify the purposes and limitations of the Organization as set forth in this Constitution. This last point is of great interest and is considered in the general observations made later on the position of the Economic and Social Council.

Article XIV also refers to the relationship between the F.A.O. and other public international organizations. The Conference is permitted to approve arrangements placing other public international organizations (for instance some institutions such as the International Institute of Agriculture (Rome),[1] the Confédération Internationale du Bois, or the Conseil International de Silviculture) dealing with questions relating to food and agriculture, under the general authority of the F.A.O. on terms agreed to between the competent authorities of the organization concerned and the F.A.O. There might even be included such regional agencies as the Middle East Agricultural Council which was established for the organization of war production in that area in World War II. It might become a Regional Council and office of the F.A.O.

The International Monetary Fund

The essential purpose of the International Monetary Fund is "to promote exchange stability, to maintain orderly exchange

---

[1] See League of Nations, *Handbook of International Organizations,* Geneva, 1938 (League of Nations Publication 1937. XII. B. 4), N. Y., Columbia University Press, Agents.

arrangements among members, and to avoid competitive exchange depreciation."[1]

Unregulated fluctuations reduce the economic specialization of countries and regions, and therefore the maximum welfare of the world and of each contributing unit. Pursuant to the special purpose of this study, it is not desired to dwell on the mechanism and procedure whereby the fluctuations of foreign exchange are kept within limits.[2] But the briefest suggestion is unavoidable. The great international regulator of international trading and investment, until World War I, was gold. It had an international value, and the structure of credit and prices in each country used to be very closely related to its holdings and anticipations of receiving gold. Debts from one country to the other that could not be settled by the export of goods, or the rendering of services, were settled by movements of gold. These movements were not necessarily direct between the debtor and creditor country, but might come through the transfer of gold acquired by trade with other nations—the movement of trade and gold was roundabout the whole globe. This gold-standard arrangement could work well only when debtors could get gold. Two difficulties arose in their attempts at acquisition. The first was that the country had to export more for gold. The second was that some countries, in a strategic position in international trade, especially the U.S.A., did not allow goods to come in for which gold could have been the payment, the tariff policy being devised mainly in the interests of some, not all, home producers. But a country could only export more if it induced its customers to buy, and the method was to *reduce its prices*, but a reduction of prices meant that its home economic

[1] See *United Nations Monetary and Financial Conference, Bretton Woods, New Hampshire, July 1 to July 22, 1944, Final Act and Related Documents,* Department of State Publication 2187; also *United Nations in the Making, Basic Documents,* World Peace Foundation, 1945.

[2] An account of this may be found in Young, J. P. *The International Economy,* N. Y., Ronald, 1942, 714 p.

structure of wages and hours was adversely affected and perhaps, too, its social services.

In other words, the home economy had to be adjusted to
the international standard. In the end this must always be
done—the real question is whether it shall be a smooth or a
rough process. In the inter-war years it became a very erratic
and disturbing process, and most nations uncoupled their
home economy wagons from the international train, because
human nature would not and could not stand catastrophically
sharp adjustments which meant unemployment, reductions
of social expenditure, social troubles regarding public assistance to the unemployed. By 1939 only the U.S.A. and Bel-
gium in the whole world worked the gold standard system.[1]
It is impossible in the present context to pursue this matter
further. Three things need emphasis: first, the dependence
of the operation of the gold standard on tariffs and therefore
international *trading* policies; secondly, the destructive effects
upon the working of the international standard of unilateral
defensive measures against depression or any other international cause (such as changes in supply, markets, new
industries) for adaptation of home structure and methods
of industries; thirdly, it accentuated the highly organized
social economy of each country, cohering around certain in-
tensely defended social principles of security, social services,
stability (neither inflation nor deflation) and full employment. A high standard of living, and the expectation of
stable and increasing welfare and income maintenance, that is,
an "expansionist" economic policy, in each country, now makes
the dependence on the "automatic" gold standard impossible
by itself. It is necessary to produce assurance, and this means
internationally provided assurance.

A regulating conference with a permanent staff is required
to administer a fund of foreign exchange. This fund is established by contributions of gold and their own currencies from

[1] Cf. League of Nations, *The Transition from War to Peace Economy*,
cited above, p. 24–6.

40

all member states. Par values of each currency must be established. The Fund may, *up to a certain point internationally determined,* check any fluctuation of a nation's exchange rates beyond certain levels above and below the par value, and such fluctuations would happen when it was over or under trading, or sharply inflating or deflating its currency. This would prevent disaster to any member from becoming disaster to all. The Fund's size, organization, and administration are directed to this purpose. There will be international consultation, the fixing of an international pattern of exchange rates, the avoidance of exchange depreciation by countries seeking advantage thereby in international competition, the redressing by short-term and limited credits of adverse movements of foreign exchange against a country. Central to the whole scheme is the obligation of every member state to give the fullest information about all the factors concerning and affecting its foreign trade position, for only where this is known to a single international brain surveying the whole field (proved up to the hilt by the chaos of the years 1928–34) can the remedial and anticipatory measures be taken. There are penalties when the Fund is abused, and higher charges for accommodation to countries which persist in a state of unbalance. By a two-thirds majority the Fund may publish a report on the economic conditions of any member country tending to produce grave international disequilibrium.

The International Monetary Fund has among its purposes, therefore, to facilitate "the expansion and balanced growth of international trade," and "the contribution thereby to the promotion and maintenance of high levels of employment and real income and to the development of the productive resources of all members as primary objectives of economic policy." It is unnecessary to discuss any further the various other functions of the Fund as stated in Article I of the Agreement, since they are instrumental to the purpose already quoted. It will immediately be observed that the purposes of the Fund as thus devised are fully correlative to one or other of the pur-

41

poses of the Food and Agriculture Organization, the I.L.O. (viz. full employment and rising standards of living), a coming world trade authority, and an international cartel authority.

It is noteworthy, that in the Final Act embodying the agreement the signatory nations especially recommend (Section VII) a number of measures which they would undertake by agreement with other agencies whose purposes are similar to those of the Fund and the Bank. This recommendation is of the highest importance to the present theme, for it is clear that the signatories believe that for the greatest effect in their own sphere the Fund and the Bank require the cooperation of good neighbors among other world institutions. The measures are:

"(1) Reduce obstacles to international trade and in other ways promote mutually advantageous international commercial relations.

"(2) Bring about the orderly marketing of staple commodities at prices fair to the producer and consumer alike.

"(3) Deal with special problems of international concern which will arise from the cessation of production for war purposes.

"(4) Facilitate by cooperative effort the harmonization of national policies of member states designed to promote and maintain high levels of employment and progressively rising standards of living."

Let it be emphasized that these recommendations are not the casual offspring of international dreamers, but the thoroughly studied conclusions of world experts.

We need not dwell on the fourth recommendation which is general and which will presumably be the field of responsibility of the Economic and Social Council. Nor need we dwell on (3) since it is transitional. Something further is said on recommendations (1) and (2) in the later sections on a World Trade Commission and Commodity Agreements and Cartels.

THE INTERNATIONAL BANK FOR RECONSTRUCTION AND DEVELOPMENT

The International Bank is a specialized agency distinct from the International Fund. While the latter is to make for stabil-

ity of currency and hence the expansion of exchange and production, the Bank's purpose is to substitute an expansionist
for a contractionist pressure on world trade. More specifically
it is to facilitate investment for productive purposes whether
for post-war reconstruction of economies destroyed or dis-
rupted by the war, or to secure reconversion or to encourage
the development of productive facilities and resources in less-
developed lands. It is to promote the long-range balanced
growth of international trade and the maintenance of equilib-
rium in balances of payments by encouraging international
investment for the development of productive resources, thus
raising productivity, the standard of living, and the conditions
of labor. It is to make or guarantee loans which will enable
a smooth transition from wartime to peacetime economy. It
may do these things, under various conditions, by guarantee-
ing, or participating in, investment made by private capital, or,
supplementing the latter, by financing productive purposes out
of its own capital. Criticism of the Bank usually sounds a
dual note, that its work could be done by private bankers
alone, and that the bankers of a single nation, for example,
the U.S.A., could manage the job.

Of course, very much international lending will continue
to be done in this way. Some, however, will be done as
planned by the creators of the World Bank, for the reasons
causing its creation: (a) the unwillingness of private investors
to lend for terms sufficiently long for execution of great works
like the T.V.A., Boulder Dam or the Sikkar Barrage in India,
and to avoid too heavy and too early a burden on the borrower's budget; (b) the unwillingness of private investors to risk
their capital in enterprises which may be of the highest indirect
value to the whole national economy, yet may not produce a
direct or tempting enough profit for that investing group. The
creation of the Bank was also commended by the unfortunate
effects of private lending in the past, and especially during the
interval between World Wars I and II. Many of the loans
were reckless—the productiveness of the economic purpose

43

was secondary to the large returns. Some borrowers played lenders against each other, and seeing the possibility of loans, contracted them without reference to the sober economic prospects of their countries, and neglected to allow for the possibility (too often realized) of a catastrophic decline in the world price of their products. Since there was no correlation between the fluctuation of currency values, international trade, and the repayment of the loans, some borrowing countries, as in Central and South America, found the debt burden in the foreign currency they could obtain had grown too large to meet, and they defaulted. The international transfer problem was out of step with lending policies. These international disharmonies were assessed by the League of Nations in the Report of the Delegation on Economic Depressions which appears in *The Transition from War to Peace Economy* in the following words: [1]

"Suddenly, after the autumn of 1929, one country after another found itself in the slough of the deepest depression in its history. For this arrest to progress, no government was prepared. No government had elaborated plans for restarting the machinery of production should occasion arise. Hurriedly, without thought for others, without international consultation, without any common leadership, each government improvised measures at first of self-defense, then of salvage. Investment ceased. The capital flow was reversed; short-term commercial loans to foreign countries were called in. Gradually the gold reserves of the debtors were sucked away in the backwash. In 1928 the United States had exported $899 million of capital; in 1929 these exports dropped to $185 million. During the ten years between 1919 and 1929 her long-term foreign investments had risen by some $9 thousand million. Europe alone had absorbed over $2.5 thousand million in this period and her total long-term indebtedness to the United States amounted to over $4.5 thousand million. Eastern and Central Europe had borrowed also large sums in the Western European capital markets. When the tap was turned on the flow of credit in 1930, these borrowers were faced with a short-term indebtedness which has been estimated at over $5 thousand million and the annual service due on the long-term debts

[1] Cited above, p. 22–3.

44

can scarcely have amounted to less than $500 million. Only a very small fraction of the total foreign capital absorbed by Central and Eastern Europe was directly invested in business in the form of share capital, the earnings on which might have been expected to decline as prosperity waned. On the rest, debt service was due, and in the two years 1930 and 1931 the prices of goods entering into international trade, of the goods by which that service had to be met, failing gold, fell by well over a third. By 1932, the annual service of debt required between 40% and 50% more goods in payment."

Further, if international lending is left to individual national governments, or private investors, rivalry results. Hostility frustrates a thoughtful common policy careful of the interests of lenders and borrowers and exacerbates national feeling, especially if the lending nation insists that the goods needed by the borrower shall be bought exclusively from it.

As emphasis has already been laid upon the relationship of the functions of the World Bank and those of other specialized agencies, repetition is unnecessary. But attention must be drawn to Article IV, Sec. 8 of Articles of Agreement of the International Bank, relating to the cooperation of the Bank and other international organizations. It directs the Bank to cooperate with the general international organization and with public international organizations having specialized responsibilities in related fields. What is of even greater interest is the second part of this section, namely, that in making decisions on applications for loans or guarantees relating to matters directly within the competence of any international organization of the types already specified, *the Bank shall give consideration to the views and recommendations of such organizations.* Certainly, the Economic and Social Council of U.N.O., the I.L.O., the F.A.O. and the Monetary Fund come to mind at once. Let it be insisted again that if some specialized agencies had not already been in existence to present views on the functions of the Bank it is highly possible that this provision would never have appeared, never have been more than a surmise in some imaginative official's mind.

45

We have already referred to the necessity of establishing a world organization for proposing ways of reducing the harm done by tariffs to the maximum potential world production and distribution. It was suggested by the Final Act of the International Monetary Conference that attention be paid to this aspect of world exchange. The currency stabilization arrangements depend upon, even as they are intended to facilitate, the foreign trade of member states. And, therefore, it must be a concern of the Fund to avert the ruin of its own stabilizing and still more its expansionist purpose by commercial practices of individual nations which set up or maintain obstacles to the free flow of goods.[1]

Much thought has already been given to the functions of such a body. There is what may be called a minimal school of thought, and another which may be called the expansionist. The minimal functions are proposed by Professor Jacob Viner.[2] They are to eliminate or substantially reduce direct controls of foreign trade. He suggests a binding convention whose signatories will be obliged:

(1) To move toward elimination of direct controls on a mutually-agreed time schedule;

(2) To define the practices which would not be permissible in the trade relations between participating countries;

(3) To formulate the procedures to be followed in common in trade relations with non-participating countries adhering to direct controls; and

[1] For an account of these practices, cf. *Commercial Policy in the Interwar Period* (League of Nations Publication 1942. II. A. 6), p. 52–60; and Committee on International Economic Policy, *Obstacles to International Trade,* N. Y. (18 Pine Street), 1945.

[2] Condliffe, J. B., and Stevenson, A., *The Common Interest in International Economic Organisation,* Montreal, International Labour Office, 1944, Studies and Reports, Series B, No. 39, p. 116.

(4) To participate in the setting up of a continuing international agency to which questions of violation of the convention, of needed revision of its terms, and of admission of new countries could be referred.

The international agency would be able to permit exemptions from the rigorous obligations assumed in exceptional cases.

Professor Alvin Hansen's proposals are wider.[1] His "International Trade Authority" would (1) promote the adoption of liberal and undiscriminatory trade practices; (2) during the post-war transition direct the flow of trade so as effectively to serve the needs of relief and reconstruction (in cooperation with other international bodies); (3) undertake a comprehensive study of long-range programs of trade policy that would contribute to general world prosperity; (4) collect information on trade policy in force in the different countries, and report on their effect on the national economy; (5) make recommendations to any member nation to modify or abandon measures it contemplates which might disrupt international trade or adversely affect the prosperity of other countries or the world in general, and this would require that no member state take action—as changes in import or export duties, or licensing, or quotas—until the international body had been informed and had a reasonable time in which to consider and formulate its recommendations.

It is clear that these functions probe deeply to the heart of national policy. It might well be that only the General Assembly itself assisted by the Economic and Social Council, acting through a special committee, would be trusted to exercise such functions, or sponsor the exercise under its immediate authority. It may be added that the International Fund required of its members (VIII, Sec. 5) information on their economy of a truly astonishing range.

[1] Hansen, Alvin E., *America's Role in the World Economy*, N. Y., Norton, 1945, Chap. 9.

There is a close natural and causal relationship between the commercial practices of individual nations and the currency relationships of the whole world. If, then, the General Assembly or the Economic and Social Council decided to be itself the body which made recommendations and proposed conventions on this most sensitive and crucial point in the world economic network, namely tariffs, it would have to have a very special and continuous relationship with the Fund.

COMMODITY AGREEMENTS AND CARTELS

Recommendation (2) of Section VII of the Final Act of the International Monetary Conference, in favor of "the orderly marketing of staple commodities at prices fair to the producer and consumer alike" leads into a very important question, usually discussed under international commodity agreements and international cartels.

Hexner shows [1] what a vast number of commodities in international trade are dominated or considerably influenced by marketing controls. These marketing controls operate through a variety of devices ranging from "gentlemen's agreements" to state monopolies, and achieve their objects by regulating exports, reserving home markets, rationing production, dividing up the market, and fixing prices and controlling stocks. The recommendation of the Monetary Conference is a recognition of the destructive economic results of the disorderly marketing of staple commodities. The evil lies in that want of coordination of supply and demand which has heretofore resulted, and cannot help resulting, in amazingly wide fluctuations of prices of staple commodities, both agricultural products, like wheat, cotton, jute, sugar, coffee, and rubber, and certain metals like copper, zinc, etc. We may quote from the Report of the Delegation on Economic Depressions of the

[1] On this see the excellent article on "International Cartels in the Post-War World," *Southern Economic Journal*, X, No. 2 (Oct. 1943), by Ervin Hexner, whose "International Steel Cartel," 1943, is a major contribution.

League of Nations (*The Transition from War to Peace Economy*, Part I, p. 23) thus:

"During the last 20 years the price of wheat and of jute has been halved three times within about twelve months, the price of cotton three times in periods of under eighteen months. The price of copper and of lead was halved four times within periods of two years and doubled three times even more rapidly. The price of zinc was halved twice in eighteen months, of tin twice in twenty-four months; zinc and lead doubled in price three times in two years or less; copper three times in eighteen months. On one occasion the price of coffee was halved in eight months, on another the price of sugar trebled in four months. Between 1920 and 1933 the price of crude rubber fluctuated between four cents a pound and twenty-five times that amount and was on several occasions doubled or halved in the space of a few months."

The injurious effects of such fluctuations are only too apparent in losses of wages and profits, employment and capital and security for all of these. These disturbances in prices and production have as their ultimate human effects "that farmers in many areas were unable to purchase clothes or boots, were unable to send their children to school for lack of them, were unable to obtain food other than that procured on the farm; that debts were unpaid and banks forced to close their doors on their depositors; that savings, large and small, were lost and the plight of the paid laborer on the farm or in the mine was often such as to make the incomeless farmer seem fortunate." [1]

Two problems of international economic collaboration arise out of the malorganization described. There is, first, the interest of both workers and employers in securing the stability and prosperity of their own industry, as a joint and as a separate interest. And, secondly, there has arisen a "national" interest in the regulation of prices and production.

The workers have already proposed International Industrial Committees for the great industries of the world such as coal,

[1] *Ibid.*, p. 24.

iron, steel, wood and textiles. They would survey the conditions and prospects of their respective industries and make recommendations for their prosperity, and attempt to secure international agreements embodying specific measures. They would be concerned with all aspects of the welfare of the industries, including production and prices, hours, minimum wages, health, social security, factory conditions and weekly rest.[1] One objective certainly would be stability, that is, steady secure employment with no disastrous reductions of prices of their goods and, therefore, of their wages, over a number of years.

It would be a most important function of the General Assembly and the Economic and Social Council, or a special body, to exert watch and ward over any restrictive tendency in the recommendations of such committees, and on the other hand to introduce a dynamic element of expansionism in production and the lowering of prices to the consumer.

On the entrepreneur's side the reasons for the establishment of cartels vary with different cartels, hence discrimination in each case is necessary. Two motivations may be crudely distinguished. One is restrictive, the establishment and use of a monopoly by a ring of producers to take advantage of the consumers. It is partly to this practice that Recommendation VII (2) of the Final Act of the Bretton Woods Conference refers. But the international cartel also seeks to avoid the disastrous effects of disorderly marketing and production of staple commodities where producers are thousands of miles away from each other, and where producers and consumers are not in adequately organized contact. The great corporations, with large invested capital needed to get the maximum returns in these industries, fight shy of abrupt assaults on their investment, interests and acquired skills by abrupt dynamic change, for being centralized they have much to lose. Technology and organization have brought this about.

[1] International Labour Conference, *Report I*, Montreal, 1944, p. 75–6; and *Official Bulletin*, XXVI, No. 1, p. 92.

If an international cartel commission were established, it would either preside at or be consulted about the formation of cartels and their modification and dissolution. It would establish a code of fair practice, to be administered by each country in which there were members of the cartel. The domestic legislation of each country, suitable to its traditions, but adequate to the modern problem, would need to include those arrangements, procedures and penalties which would give effect to the code. Among these would certainly be a power of investigation into and publicity of the transactions of the members of those cartels.

Secondly, there is another aspect of the cartel, as is shown in the emergence of international commodity agreements made between states in the interwar years on wheat, sugar, tea, coffee, beef, timber, tin and rubber. Their purpose has been to regulate the production and the marketing of these commodities, in order that some standard of accepted welfare of those in the industry, and of the general welfare of the nations of import and export, may be established which is compatible with fair dealing with the consumers of those commodities, and yet does not leave the prosperity of the nation and the fiscal arrangements of the state vulnerable to sudden shocks. States have been as interested in the establishment of these agreements as private producers and consumers, because they must maintain standards of welfare and security, and producers and consumers need their authority to support their claims in the framework of the nation's welfare as a whole. Particularly since the onset of the Great Depression intergovernmental raw material control schemes (i.e. international commodity agreements) were established by the principal countries of purchase and production. Thus, sugar, tea, coffee, beef, timber, tin, rubber; and others have been suggested, including copper, cotton, coal, sisal.[1]

[1] Cf. Rowe, J. W. F., *Markets and Men* (N. Y., Macmillan, 1936); Hodson, H. V., *Slump and Recovery, 1929–1937* (N. Y., Oxford Univ. Press, 1938); Staley, Eugene, *Raw Materials in Peace and War* (N. Y.

A world international cartel and commodity agreement authority must then have regard to the interests of both producers and consumers of the particular commodity for which a world arrangement is made.[1] It must, however, also be concerned with the effect of its decisions upon all the other economic sectors and nations within the economic framework. Not only would the workers who produce the commodity for which there is an international arrangement suffer if there were no such organization, and be affected by its ruling if it came into existence, but all other producers and consumers would feel the effects of anything authoritatively decided by any publicly-controlled commodity organization.

Six problems would face an organization regulating a specific commodity and would certainly, and in a much higher and important degree, confront a world institution with power to supervise and regulate all cartel activities. Without discussion, they are listed, because this at once draws attention to the interrelationship between these activities and those of other economic bodies. The problems are:

(1) to secure adequate supplies and prices giving an acceptable and stable return to the *efficient* producer;

(2) "to further the enjoyment by all states, great and small, victor and vanquished to access on equal terms to the trade and to the raw materials of the world which are needed for their economic prosperity," [2] and to recommend action on "strategic materials";

(3) to relate cartel policy to anti-depression measures, to the currency stabilization functions of the World Fund,

Council on Foreign Relations, 1937), as of outstanding interest on this subject. A good survey of the problems and solutions hitherto attempted by governments, together with an opulent bibliography, appears in the I.L.O. publication entitled *Intergovernmental Commodity Agreements* (1944)—the texts of the agreements are there reproduced.

[1] *Commercial Policy in the Post-war World,* cited above, especially Chaps. VI and VII.

[2] Atlantic Charter, Article IV, see *United Nations in the Making: Basic Documents,* Boston, World Peace Foundation, 1945.

and cushioning the great primary industries against erratic and severe fluctuations of price and production by the building up of "buffer stocks";

(4) to coordinate its price and production policy with the I.L.O.'s concern for social security and the social services;

(5) to foster the adaptability of labor and capital to new demands and to changing methods of supply technique, and not tolerate stagnation in security;

(6) to resist any freezing of the economic fate of the various countries of the world as it stands at this moment, especially the so-called "colonial" economy or "raw" material economies, and to cooperate with the International Bank for Reconstruction and Development and the Food and Agriculture Organization in carrying out a liberal and expansionist policy which furthers the development of backward countries.

Educational and Cultural Organization of the United Nations

It is not the present object to enter into the detail of the purposes and constitution of an International Education Organization. But a few words must be said about its relationship to the rest of the agencies. Its fundamental purpose is to develop mutual understanding and appreciation of the life and culture of the peoples of the world and to develop the idea that all citizens of any country are citizens of the whole world, with obligations to further the best morality known to our time, as it concerns the maintenance of peace and the promotion of international justice. And a cognate purpose would be furtherance of a consciousness of the economic and social interconnections of all nations and all people.

Representatives of the United Nations are meeting in London (November 1945) to consider the establishment of an Educational and Cultural Organization of the United Nations. They have before them a Draft Constitution prepared by an earlier conference of Allied Ministers of Education. In the Preamble to this Draft appear the following significant statements of purpose:

"Recognizing that cooperation in education and the furtherance of cultural interchange in the arts, the humanities and the sciences will promote the freedom, the dignity and the well-being of all and therefore assist in the attainment of understanding, confidence, security and peace among the peoples of the world;

"Dedicated to the proposition that the free and unrestricted education of the peoples of the world, and the free and unrestricted exchange among them of ideas and knowledge are essential to the advancement of human welfare and to the preservation of security and peace." [1]

Such an agency was needed by the League of Nations, but the Intellectual Cooperation Organization established under the Covenant was not strong enough for the mission which lay before it. The weakness was, in part, intentional. There were countries which did not wish education in international obligations and interdependence. Indeed, there were some who voted for the exclusion from the draft Covenant of a phrase which might have given rise to a real department concerned with the fostering of a consciousness of world integration and loyalty. Perhaps after World War II there will be less reluctance to give rein to such an organization. The Educational and Cultural Organization now proposed can be of the greatest assistance to the United Nations and the special agencies, by making a central part of its teaching a doctrine of world interdependence in matters economic and social, and showing by a multitude of literary and graphic devices how important and strong are these threads, even though to the unassisted eye they are invisible. In order that it may be of the greatest possible aid, it would need to be in intimate contact with the various agencies, which would supply the expert data, and which might well be able to suggest methods

[1] From the Preamble of the Draft Constitution for an Educational and Cultural Organization of the United Nations, Department of State, *Bulletin*, XII, p. 168.

of argument, exposition and persuasion derived from their professional insight into the problems involved. For the education authority there would be the great and exacting task of discovering and using all the many techniques of visual representation, as also the exchange of scholars and teachers and students. Many of those who took part in the establishment of the new agencies were, about fifteen or twenty years ago, exchange scholars in the countries which were the principal parties to the new multilateral agreements designed to knit the world together. Two decades ago the now established network of mind with mind had already begun to be fashioned.

Articles XIII and XIV of the draft Constitution of the Education and Cultural Organization concerns itself with the relations between itself and other public international organizations. They prescribe: [1]

"ARTICLE XIII, *Relations with the United Nations*

"1. The Organization shall be brought in relationship with the United Nations, this relationship to be defined by an agreement approved by the appropriate organs of both bodies.

"2. Notwithstanding the provisions of Article XI, such agreement may, if approved by the Conference by a two-thirds majority, involve modification of the provisions of this Constitution, provided that no such agreement shall modify the purposes and limitations of the Organization.

"ARTICLE XIV, *Relations with Other Specialized International Organizations*

"1. The Organization may cooperate with other specialized international organizations, both public and private, whose interest and activities are related to and in harmony with its purposes.

"2. The Executive Board, with the approval of the Conference, may enter into agreements with the competent authorities of such organizations defining the distribution of responsibilities and methods of cooperating, and maintain such joint committees with them as may be necessary to assure effective cooperation.

---

[1] Draft Constitution for an Educational and Cultural Organization of the United Nations, *ibid.*, p. 172.

"3. Whenever the Conference of this Organization and the competent authorities of any other organization whose purposes are similar deem it desirable to effect transfer of the resources and functions of the latter to this Organization, the Executive Board, subject to the approval of the Conference, may enter into mutually acceptable arrangements for this purpose."

The general objectives of a world economic policy have now been clarified, and the specific need for planned cooperation among the special agencies of international economic and social action examined. It is now necessary to relate these findings to the provisions of the United Nations Charter.

CHAPTER III

CHARTER PROVISIONS FOR AN ECONOMIC AND SOCIAL COUNCIL

THE provisions of the United Nations Charter for the promotion of international cooperation in the economic and social fields are to be found in Article 1, paragraph 3; Articles 13, 17 and 18; and the whole of Chapters IX and X. A commentary is necessary as a foundation for subsequent discussion of the future fulfillment of the purposes of the Charter.

Among the purposes stated in Article 1 is the following: "to achieve international cooperation in solving international problems of an economic, social, cultural, or humanitarian character." This phrase, appearing where it does, is of appreciable significance, because it vests in the *whole* Organization, as distinct from any one of its special organs, the general purpose it states. This is a purpose, then, not merely of the General Assembly or of the Security Council or of the Economic and Social Council, but also of the Organization as a whole. This needs to be noted, because in the division of functions between the General Assembly and the Security Council, the Charter clearly and unreservedly assigns to the General Assembly the consideration of the general principles of cooperation, the discussion of questions relating to the maintenance of international peace and security (Articles 10, 11), and the special responsibility for promoting international economic and social cooperation (Article 13, par. 1 (b)). The Security Council has no specific duties and rights regarding international economic and social cooperation. But concern for the world balance of power will certainly impel the permanent members of the Security Council to seek to exercise an influence on world economic policy, though not necessarily in the name of the Security Council.

ROLE OF THE GENERAL ASSEMBLY

The initial responsibility in connection with the promotion of economic and social cooperation is placed upon the General Assembly, in the following terms: [1]

"The General Assembly shall initiate studies and make recommendations for the purpose of: . . . promoting international cooperation in political, economic, social, cultural, educational and health fields. . . ."

In Chapter IX, on International Economic and Social Cooperation, the Charter describes the functions of the Organization as follows:

"With a view to the creation of conditions of stability and well-being which are necessary for peaceful and friendly relations among nations based on respect for the principle of equal rights and self-determination of peoples, the United Nations shall promote:

a. higher standards of living, full employment, and conditions of economic and social progress and development;
b. solutions of international economic, social, health and related problems; and international cultural and educational cooperation; and
c. universal respect for, and observance of, human rights and fundamental freedoms for all without distinction as to race, sex, language, or religion."

The responsibility for the discharge of the functions of the Organization as set forth in the Charter, that is, the above program, and the instrumental actions required by it, shall be vested in the General Assembly and, "under the authority of the General Assembly, in the Economic and Social Council, which shall have for this purpose the powers set forth in Chapter X," to be discussed shortly. Among the powers instrumental to its main purposes, as stated in Chapter IX, is that of bringing into relationship with the Organization the spe-

[1] Chap. IV, Art. 13, 1(b).

cialized agencies and the initiation of negotiations for the creation of any new specialized agencies.

There is another responsibility vested in the General Assembly; under Article 17, paragraph 3, it "shall consider and approve any financial and budgetary arrangements with specialized agencies referred to in Article 57 (that is the economic, social and other international bodies set up by intergovernmental agreements) and shall examine the administrative budgets of such specialized agencies with a view to making recommendations to the agencies concerned."

Furthermore, it is the General Assembly which elects the Economic and Social Council.

The general features of these provisions need some consideration. The General Assembly is in nowise a sovereign, governing body, exercising peremptory authority over either single states or groups of states or over existing or future world agencies. Indeed in the proceedings leading up to the final draft, members of the Conference made it clear that Article 2, paragraph 7 of the Charter governed all other provisions of the Charter. Consequently, the General Assembly has no authority to intervene in matters which are essentially within the domestic jurisdiction of any state. What the evolution of many years will yet produce, it is unnecessary for the moment to consider, and what is the meaning of "essentially" history has yet to tell. The present provisions, undoubtedly founded upon the experience of the League's economic and social agencies in the interwar years, and upon a consideration of what at this stage of world consciousness is feasible, do not go any further than the initiation of studies, the making of recommendations and the coordination of policies *in accordance with specific agreements yet to be made* between the specialized agencies and the Organization. There is no suggestion whatever of the imposition of an independent plan. On the contrary, the maximum authority given is the *promotion* of international cooperation by the specific means of studies and recommendations. In the Dumbarton Oaks draft, the word "facilitation" was used. Under the terms of Article 14, the Assembly is given power to recommend measures for the *adjustment* of situations likely to impair the general welfare. Thus, *promotion* and *adjustment*, by *studies* and *recommendations*, are the central core of the provisions regarding economic and social matters.

However, it should be noticed that though there is a heavy limitation on the force of the General Assembly's authority, there is no limitation, apart from the safeguarding of domestic jurisdiction, upon its scope. Its scope is unconfined, and rightly so, for any single sector of economic and social life may get out of order and disturb and subvert all other sectors everywhere. The lesson of the famous sequence has been well-learned: Hawley-Smoot tariff; protest of a score of nations who were America's foreign customers and suppliers; retaliation by them; loss of foreign trade and employment by all; the deepening of the depression in the U.S.A.; the fall in its foreign purchasing power; the decline of overseas national economies, and mass unemployment; panic in central Europe; the flight from the gold standard in Great Britain and other countries; defensive measures by almost every individual country all in terms of restricting foreign trade (especially imports) which would cause them to lose gold and foreign currency; and therefore the reduction of foreign trade by quotas, prohibitions, currency controls, investment restrictions, etc., and so the increase of unemployment elsewhere by the repression of the demand for the goods of others.[1]

Also, no single specialized economic world agency can be fully utilized to the maximum of its value to humanity, unless the Assembly has power to assist it, not only in regard to its own specific functions, but in regard to the functions performed by other agencies in the remaining economic and social sectors.

As we have seen, the specialized agencies already in exist-

[1] See issues of League of Nations *World Economic Survey* for the years, 1931–32, 1932–33, 1933–34, N. Y., Columbia Univ. Press, Agents.

ence or contemplated, do not fully cover the whole range of functions necessary for international economic and social cooperation. In the interim period, which might be long, until the establishment of such bodies, the General Assembly would need to fulfill the very important function of making studies and recommendations on the subjects which such bodies would deal with if they existed; and of proposing to the existing agencies such additions to or modifications of their authority and practice as would fill the gap; and, finally, of proposing the establishment of new agencies. It is clear that the Assembly, being a general forum of discussion, and a center of studies, will always be a dynamic factor, and always a place where the residuary power of proposal and initiative is lodged, so long as the specialized agencies have not been set up. And even if the whole field were already covered by the specialized agencies the Assembly's plenary power, qualified by the non-coercive nature of the authority given it, would be a dynamic creative element.

The approval of the General Assembly is required for agreements defining the relationships of the various specialized agencies to the United Nations Organization. This imposes both a responsibility and a duty upon the General Assembly to make sure that such agreements fully utilize the services both of the agencies and of the Economic and Social Council, and foster the most fruitful relationship between the specialized agencies themselves. The General Assembly is the engine of dynamic development. This is as it should be, because in the Assembly all states are represented, and each member, whatever his stage of civilization, economic progress, or population, has an equal title to speak and vote. In view of the evident supremacy of the Assembly, much more marked than in the Dumbarton Oaks Proposals, it is rather surprising to find the Economic and Social Council elevated to the status of "principal organ," standing in Article 7 on the same level with the Security Council, the General Assembly, the Trusteeship Council, the International Court of Justice and a Secretariat. However, its promotion in status was evidence of a very general recognition of the importance of the international economic function.

Functions of the Council

The Economic and Social Council may make or initiate studies and reports with respect to international economic, social, cultural, educational, health and related matters and may make recommendations with respect to any such matters to the General Assembly, to the Members of the United Nations, and to the specialized agencies concerned. It may make recommendations for the purpose of promoting respect for, and observance of, human rights and fundamental freedoms for all. It may prepare draft conventions for submission to the General Assembly, with respect to matters falling within its competence. It may call, in accordance with the rules prescribed by the United Nations, international conferences on matters falling within its competence.

At this stage it is essential to underline the evident intention of the Charter to keep centered in the specialized bodies the responsibility for their own special fields, and not to encroach upon that responsibility. Presently, we shall be concerned with the manner in which the Assembly and the Economic and Social Council ought to act, if they are to discharge advantageously their responsibilities. One of those principles of action must concern the extent to which the Economic and Social Council should interfere with the exercise of the special responsibilities of the specialized agencies.

What the relationship between the Organization and the specialized agencies is to be has to be settled by agreement (Articles 57, 63) between the Economic and Social Council and the agencies, and such agreements are subject to the approval of the General Assembly. This implies the formulation of a relationship, a general pattern of distributed authority and initiative, between the Assembly, the Economic and Social Council and specialized agencies. Before turning to this extremely important theme it is necessary to consider a few other provisions of the Charter so that the total picture may be recognized.

First, the Economic and Social Council which will thus operate as the continuing deputed council of the Assembly is to consist of representatives of 18 members of the Organization. Proposals made in Committee to allocate fixed proportions of the places to chief industrial states, or the Big Five, or to regions, were rejected. So also was one that *all* members of the Assembly should be members of the Council. The Council as it is now constituted is big enough to satisfy, if not all the member nations, then the principal ones, and to give representation to regional blocs. To include more members, and there will always be a pressure tending to equate the numbers of the Economic and Social Council with the total membership of the Assembly, would be to risk frustrating vigorous and coherent discussion and action. The Governing Body of the International Labor Organization has thirty-two members, of which 16 represent governments. The total number is so large by reason of the I.L.O.'s peculiar tripartite method of representation. In practice, this has not proved to be too unwieldy. Hence, if there were heavy pressure for the increase in numbers in the size of the Economic and Social Council, although it would be undesirable to arrive at thirty-two, some latitude might nevertheless be allowed. The states so represented are elected by the General Assembly by two-thirds vote for three years; six states are elected each year, thus providing both movement and continuity. Each member has one representative with one vote, and decisions are taken by a simple majority of those present and voting. This requires no special commentary.

We must, however, look with some care at the functions and powers attributed to the Economic and Social Council. (a) It is empowered (Article 66, paragraph 1) to carry out, within the scope of its competence, general recommendations of the General Assembly. (b) It has the power (Article 62, paragraphs 1, 2, and 4) to make recommendations on its own initiative with respect to international economic, social and other humanitarian matters, and prepare draft conventions for submission to the General Assembly, and to call international conferences. (c) Another responsibility (Article 64) is to obtain regular reports from the economic, social and other specialized organizations and agencies brought into relationship with the Organization, and to coordinate their activities through consultations with and recommendations to them. (d) It may communicate its observations on these reports to the General Assembly. (e) It may furnish information to the Security Council and must assist the Security Council upon its request. (f) It may, with the approval of the General Assembly, perform services at the request of members of the United Nations and at the request of specialized agencies.

Some observations on these powers are necessary at this point. Evidently, regular and continuous leadership will be exercised by the Economic and Social Council through studies and recommendations, coordination, and the initiation of international conferences. The Council will receive proposals and consider or refer them to the proper technical section.

Three things may be observed with reference to the Council's position. The power to receive and discuss regular reports from the specialized agencies is valueless without the authority to secure them. They are to be obtained by "appropriate steps" (Article 64) as a result of amicable representation. Their form must be most suitable to the function for the fulfillment of which the Economic and Social Council is responsible. This implies an obligation on the part of the specialized agencies which has not yet been clearly established. Article 64 provides also that the Council may make arrangements with the Members of the United Nations and the specialized agencies to obtain reports on measures they have taken to give effect to recommendations made by the Council or the General Assembly.

Properly implemented, the power to require and consider reports may be, as the history of national governmental administration has shown, a very potent factor in the development of control over the specialized agencies. The practice is well-known of calling for reports from the departments in Washington as it is in the government of every other civilized nation. Even more, the beneficial effect of relating the activities of a specialized body to the general welfare may be seen, for example, in the relationship of the various government departments to the Congressional committees; and even more cogently, in the case of public corporations like TVA, who come to the Congress and its committees for appropriations, and who, in any case, appropriations or not, are subject to investigation by the committees. It is, perhaps, too early in the development of world agencies to expect the nations which have created such organizations as the I.L.O., the Food and Agriculture Organization, the International Fund and the International Bank, to oblige the agencies to submit their administration to the occasional investigatory power of the Economic and Social Council. Some day that may come and, employed not as interference but reasonably in the interests of the effective performance of the functions of the agencies, this power of investigation could well be the instrument of progress. It is to be noticed that these agencies are to have their activities coordinated through consultations between the Economic and Social Council and themselves. Recommendations, too, may be made by the Council to them and the General Assembly. Their force will, in the early years, be a function of the wisdom and the administrative tact of the Council.

ADMINISTRATIVE BUDGETS OF SPECIALIZED AGENCIES

The provision for the examination of the administrative budgets of the agencies with a view to making recommendations to them is undoubtedly the product of a body of opinion which has grown rapidly from about 1941. For it then began to be appreciated that a fairly large number of world agencies would be required; that each of them would administer substantial sums of money; and that, therefore, waste and overlapping might be avoided only if some outside body surveyed all the budgets in relation to each other. But the power to review the budgets of the specialized agencies was given directly to the Economic and Social Council in the Dumbarton Oaks Proposals. Under the Charter it is no longer an original power of the Economic and Social Council, but belongs to the General Assembly.

The problem of the relationship between the budgets of the specialized agencies to each other, and to a coordinating body, was the direct offspring of the relationship between the League of Nations and the International Labor Organization. In pursuance of Article 13, paragraph 2 of the I.L.O. Constitution,[1] the budget of the I.L.O. was sanctioned after consideration, examination and vote by the League Assembly. The League Assembly acted on the report of its Committee (Fourth) on Finance, and this again acted after the receipt of the proposals transmitted to it by the Secretary-General as the result of the earlier investigations and report of the Supervisory Commission (with a membership of seven elected by the Assembly for 3 years and eligible for re-election), which, of course, had made a direct personal inquiry into the estimates submitted by the Director of the I.L.O. after sanction by his own Governing Body.[2] The League of Nations received from the Member States contributions, not only for

[1] "Each of the Members will pay the traveling and subsistence expenses of its Delegates and their advisers and of its Representatives attending the meetings of the Conference or Governing Body, as the case may be.

"All the other expenses of the International Labor Office and of the meetings of the Conference or Governing Body shall be paid to the Director by the Secretary-General of the League of Nations out of the General funds of the League.

"The Director shall be responsible to the Secretary-General of the League for the proper expenditure of all moneys paid to him in pursuance of this article."

[2] Cf. I.L.O., Report I, International Labor Conference, 26th Session, 1944, Chap. II, for description.

itself, but for the I.L.O. to whom it passed on a share of the total payments made by the Member States. For a strong, active, creative and independent kind of organization like the I.L.O., this was a rather restrictive relationship, and many people within and outside the organization proposed from time to time complete financial autonomy. In December 1943, the Workers' Group proposed and the Governing Body agreed that the subject of "financial autonomy" should be considered by the forthcoming Conference. The Workers' Group wanted authority for the I.L.O. to adopt its own budget, collect its money directly, and lend and hold capital as its members directly determined. Thus they believed the I.L.O. would function more effectively. But the problem arose that the I.L.O. would, in the future, be only one of a number of world agencies; if it could make a case for autonomy, what would stop all the others? It was feared that the contributing nations would have no central organization able to check expenditures and induce economy: [1]

"If, as seems probable, a number of new international agencies are set up, some machinery of consultation between all of them, in order to avoid the friction and waste which would result from divergent administrative practices and competition in recruitment, is clearly desirable. Thus, the fundamental problem which the League procedure was designed to solve is likely to take on a much wider aspect, for which the old machinery must necessarily prove inadequate. . . . Eventually, no doubt, an international budget and the necessary machinery for its effective operation will be devised and operated. But until the general set-up of international agencies is known — their number, their scope, their membership, their degree of control over policy, the success with which they succeed in operating, and the support or otherwise they receive from public opinion —it would seem wiser to proceed by the series of practical steps which appear most appropriate during the creative and experimental stage. As pointed out elsewhere in this Report, the approach now being made to providing the world with the necessary international agencies is gradual and functional. The choice of such an approach is deliberate and its advantages are manifest. Many of

[1] *Ibid.*, p. 163, 166.

these advantages would be lost and the whole prospect of success might indeed be prejudiced if a centralized system of finance based on insufficient experience were introduced at too early a stage. This does not imply of course that co-ordination should be wholly lacking. The necessity for consultation between international agencies on their common financial and administrative problems is, as already indicated, obvious. Moreover, an important form of co-ordination functions automatically at the national level. The delegates representing a country in a series of international agencies draw their instructions from and report back to a common authority in which the policies they advocate or the activities they approve are the result of interdepartmental discussion and agreement. It is as the result of this co-ordination that the various international agencies will first be able to discover the scale, extent, and intensity of their operations and this experience will provide the basis on which co-ordination at the international level can subsequently be soundly constructed."

Thus, even while pleading for gradualness and against centralization of financial provision, it could not but be admitted that a coordination of functions is necessary in the interest of the total pattern of world economic activity. We must again emphasize, in the interest, even no less, of the specific functions of each agency.

One of the most effective instruments of governmental co-ordination, as well as of economy, is the unified budget. This is the strong case for the retention of the budgetary power of the League of Nations, as a "roof" organization over a whole family of specialized agencies. The administrative value of a financial coordinating authority depends on the authority it exercises. In the present Charter, not the Economic and Social Council but the General Assembly has the power to examine the "administrative budgets," and to make recommendations to specific agencies. The Charter does not clarify the nature of the recommendations, and does not qualify the word "recommendations" by anything which discloses what force would be attributed to them. But it is not an accident that the word "budget" was not used, but, instead, simply the phrase "administrative budget"? The qualifying word "administrative" suggests that the Assembly will concern itself with what each organization spends on its own management, that is to say, personnel, property, offices and apparatus and not the funds which it has to manage or disburse for its function. Thus, in the case of the International Bank for Reconstruction and Development, the General Assembly would presumably not be concerned with the policies and financial commitments incurred in making loans, but would be concerned with the cost of the secretariat, the renting of headquarters, the sending out of missions, the appointment of consultants, and such like items. That, at least, is a reasonable deduction from the phrase "*administrative* budget." Yet, as the relationship between the United States Reconstruction Finance Corporation and the United States Bureau of the Budget demonstrates, the power of the surveying organization over the specialized agency, using the administrative budget alone, can, in fact, be utilized for a more thoroughgoing investigation than the former suggests. This is no doubt why, between Dumbarton Oaks and San Francisco, it was realized that the authority should be that of the Assembly. This could clearly delegate the authority formally and substantially to the Economic and Social Council; and there is little doubt that it will. The power of financial supervision gives the central and coordinating body invaluable information about the success or failure of specialized agencies. It goes far beyond mere administrative matters to which its attention is in the first place directed, for these matters require explanation, and can usually be justified only by reference to expenditures on functions. Budget information might well supplement the reports the Economic and Social Council may require. However, there is still the question of principle: at what degree of control over management and operations ought the Assembly and its instrument, the Economic and Social Council, to aim, and for the achievement of what international purposes? To that question we return at a later stage, saying here only this: if the Assembly and the Economic and Social Council have no direct responsibility

69

for the success of the everyday work of the specialized agencies, it must be extremely careful not to enfeeble their financial independence.

COORDINATION OF ACTIVITIES

Only two other things need mention at this stage. In the Dumbarton Oaks Proposals, the coordination of international activities in economic and social matters was dependent upon a relationship between the General Assembly, the Economic and Social Council and the several specialized agencies. It is remarkable that a party to the coordinating arrangements under the Charter is, in addition, "the Members of the United Nations," in certain cases. Notably this applies to the power of the Economic and Social Council to obtain regular reports —it may take steps to obtain them from the Members of the United Nations as well as the international agencies. It applies to measures for the coordination of the activities of the specialized agencies, directly by consultation and recommendations, and through recommendation to the General Assembly, and, which is extremely important and interesting, through recommendations to "the Members of the United Nations." Must such recommendations go to *all* the Members simultaneously? They might very fruitfully be addressed to any one Member if that is suitable; or some. And, again, the Council may perform services at the request of Members of the United Nations. The importance of these new dispositions will be discussed later.

Finally, the subject of international economic and social activity (particularly it may be said with regard to the promotion of higher standards of living, full employment, and conditions of economic and social progress and development), was regarded as so urgent and important, that, pledged as the United Nations were by Article 2, paragraph 2 to fulfill the obligations of the Charter in good faith, they repeated in Article 56 this pledge for international economic and social cooperation. Thus: "All Members pledge themselves to take

70

joint and separate action in cooperation with the Organization for the achievement of the purposes set forth in Article 55." Why this pledge was required and given will be fully realized later.

Arrangements with Agencies for Joint Deliberations

By Article 69 the Economic and Social Council is empowered to make arrangements for representatives of the specialized agencies to participate without vote in its deliberations and in its commissions, and for its representatives to participate in the deliberations of the specialized agencies. Also by Article 69 (partly as a sop to those who were anxious about the restricted membership of the Council) the Council must invite any Member to participate without vote, in its deliberations, on any matter of particular concern to that Member. It is clear that the participation of the representatives of the specialized organizations in the deliberations of the Economic and Social Council would be not only desirable but necessary. It may be recalled that in the relationships between the I.L.O. and the League of Nations: (a) the Director of the International Labor Office had the right (frequently used) to occupy a seat in the Council of the League whenever matters of concern to the I.L.O. were discussed; (b) so also in the Assembly and its committees, the right being especially important and practical in regard to the latter; (c) the Governing Body had the right to approach the Council and Assembly on any matter, received and examined League documents and decisions, and took appropriate action to cooperate and make valuable observations; (d) the I.L.O. had special representation at the great conferences such as the World Economic Conference of 1927 and the Monetary and Economic Conference of 1933; and (e) it had special representation on the League Committees of Public Works, of Refugees, on Economic Depressions, and on the Permanent Mandates Commission.

However able and representative the members of the Economic and Social Council, however continuous their study

71

of the world agencies and the problems in general of world development, however well qualified the secretariat which would be necessary to help the Economic and Social Council, the experience of the League of Nations and of the internal government in any of the larger and more economically advanced member states demonstrates beyond a shadow of a doubt the necessity of direct representation of the special functional bodies. For they have two contributions indispensable to right action. One is their knowledge, and the second is the vigor and intensity of their interest in the result. Much of the coordinating activity of the Economic and Social Council, which must appear to specialized agencies as rather fussy and a little unnecessary, will depend for its effectiveness on proposing recommendations which have a chance of being promptly and amicably accepted and carried out. This will not be absolutely guaranteed if the specialized agencies are consulted in the preparatory stages of such recommendations, but it is almost a certainty that if they were *not* consulted, policy would be conceived in ignorance, received with suspicion, and treated with prejudice. This representation of the agencies in the Economic and Social Council and of the Council in the agencies is of cardinal importance, and no sense of amour propre should deter the Council from seeking, and almost beseeching, the participation of the specialized agencies, and, therefore, of making such procedural concessions as will produce a happy working arrangement.

Establishment of Economic Commissions

The Charter (Article 68) provides that the Economic and Social Council should set up commissions in the economic field and such other commissions as may be required. It does not stipulate as did the original Proposals that these commissions should consist of experts. The Charter gives no further clue to the detail of the arrangements and machinery it implies. But at Dumbarton Oaks it was prescribed that the commissions should consist of experts. At San Francisco it was asked whether they should consist of experts only, or whether mixed commissions of experts and others of political and representative character, or only of the officials of different governments where action was urgent might not be better from case to case? The field was therefore left open to the dictates of need and the lessons of experience.

Perhaps it is intended that the Commissions should be composed and operate rather like the Technical Organizations of the League of Nations. These Technical Organizations—for example, the Economic and Financial Organization, the Communications and Transit Organization, the Health Organization, the Intellectual Cooperation Organization—were not either wholly consultative and advisory bodies or wholly executory bodies. They were hybrid, though they were more consultative than executory. Operating under statutory resolutions of the League Council, which gave them their authority and terms of reference, these Organizations made no decisions which were at once obligations upon the Member States. Obligations were assumed only through votes in the League Council or the Assembly, or in most cases by special international multilateral conventions. But before such action could be taken, usually, by the League Assembly and Council, or a convention adopted, perhaps as the result of the calling of a special conference of states for the purpose, a long and arduous preparatory process was required, comprising research, the marshalling of information, the sifting of statistics, the compilation of laws and analysis of laws and administrative experience and records, discussion among experts and the canvassing of national opinion, the formulation of proposals, and the consummation of draft recommendations or conventions. Such Organizations were served by the League Secretariat, which thus provided some articulating liaison between the several Organizations and the League as a whole, and between the functions of the several Organizations.

This is not the appropriate place to discuss in any detail their personnel and composition. But, briefly, they were composed of men of diverse nationalities, for representative purposes, but chosen on account of their personal technical qualifications appropriate for the organization's function, or because they were key officials in those administrative departments of their national governments having a direct relationship with the functions of the League Organization. Thus, as a result of deliberate theory (to which we refer later), it was contrived that these consultative bodies might be not merely preparers of policy and conventions. For each member was also able to take back from the international committees to his own nation, and his own administrative office, a direct knowledge of the international agreements reached, and was in a good position to get the agreement carried out or to get public opinion prepared for the future.

What the Commissions proposed by the Charter would do, having regard to the fact that on the one hand, there is the Council itself, and on the other the whole series of permanent international functional agencies, it is difficult to surmise. Most likely they will be advisory and exploratory, acting as the continuous, mediating and constructive agencies on the one hand, preparing material, detailed reports and proposals for the Economic and Social Council; and, on the other hand, distributing to the operating international agencies the decisions of the Council, and perhaps even formulating them in more elaborate and concrete form. Where the necessary international agencies are not yet set up, let us say, for tariff and cartel matters, there the Commissions would function, much as the Economic and Financial Organization of the League, to prepare and knit together international collaboration, eventuating in conferences and even perhaps treaties, but certainly always as illuminators of the desirable and feasible international standard.

The Secretariat

A permanent staff is, of course, essential to the operation of any continuing international organization, for reasons of space and time stand in the way of permanent sessions of representatives of the member states, and world-famed experts can be available for only part of the time. It would be possible for the Commissions to have their own separate staffs, but it is obviously better that their staffs, as also the staff of the Economic and Social Council, should be part of the United Nations Secretariat.

Chapter XV of the Charter provides for a Secretariat, headed by a Secretary-General who is to be the chief administrative officer of the Organization. This ramifies throughout the Organization, bringing an instrument of permanent coordination and cohesion into its complicated system of councils. The Secretary-General is to be appointed by the General Assembly on the recommendation of the Security Council. The truly important feature of his functions is that he is to act as Secretary-General at all meetings of the General Assembly, the Security Council, the Economic and Social Council and the Trusteeship Council. He would be the administrative stem around which the political and governmental functions and administrative leadership of these bodies revolved. To them, he would bring a knowledge of all the work being undertaken by the Assembly and Councils and their committees and the commissions and administrative departments. He could be a momentous influence on the operation of any part of the entire machinery.

Appointed by the Secretary-General under the regulations established by the General Assembly, there will be a great body of permanent officials—the international secretariat, or civil service. The Charter requires (Article 101, paragraph 2) that "appropriate staffs shall be permanently assigned to the Economic and Social Council, the Trusteeship Council, and, as required, to other organs of the United Nations. These staffs shall form a part of the Secretariat." This amply provides for the necessary specialization of the staff; and yet affords both that connection with the whole Organization, which is important for a sense of loyalty to the over-all purposes of the Organization, and a basis for transfers from department to department of the Organization as the abilities and inclination of the official suggest. The specialization of the staff for the functions of the Economic and Social Council is a necessity of the highest order. The work that must be done in the various branches of world economic and social policy—let us say, the liaison with any one of the specialized agencies—requires a life-long devotion if all the profundities, detail and insight, which make for successful advice and creativeness, are to be brought to assist the fulfillment of the purposes of the General Assembly and the Economic and Social Council.

CHAPTER IV

THE TASKS OF THE GENERAL ASSEMBLY AND THE ECONOMIC AND SOCIAL COUNCIL

ENOUGH has now been said to establish beyond a doubt the necessity for a close working relationship between the several special functional world agencies of economic and social development, and to demonstrate the need of a coordinating, initiating and supplementing activity on the part of the Economic and Social Council and, above it, of the General Assembly.

What has really been demonstrated is the necessity of a single economic and social world mind. World government implies a world mind, even as a world mind is a condition of a world government. It is not desired however in the slightest degree to suggest the need for anything like a superstate or even at this stage a fairly highly organized world federation. The limitation in the Charter regarding "domestic jurisdiction" is sufficiently peremptory. All that is meant is that, if the spontaneous interconnections between nation and nation, and economic occupations in the various parts of the world, were developed and extended with the interest of the maximum welfare of the whole world as the goal, one mighty, capacious brain, surveying the whole, could be an instrument of great progress. In fact, such a thing will forever be impossible, and it most certainly is at this stage of the world's development. Even more, progress through government is dependent not merely upon intellectual comprehension by one mind, but also upon the will or desire that there shall be union, and today that is only in its very early stages. Instead of one mind, a series of individual special agencies in each of which is vested a special function arose, each in its own time. That was historically unavoidable, just as it was historically unavoidable for the departments of the U. S. Government or of Great Britain or of France to grow up in the capital cities at different times and without a coordinated pattern, or at the beginning, any completeness of organization or function in each separate department.

Therefore, it is essential to introduce into the historical and sporadic growth of world departments the unifying, harmonizing and energizing influence of a coordinating body with special authority. All sectors of economic and social endeavor, do, in fact, constitute a *natural* unity. They are not even a collective: but they begin as one thing. It is only historical accident, and the incapacity of mankind to do everything at once at an early stage of development, that has caused one, two, three or more individual agencies to be separately established. Furthermore, even when more of these are developed, each of them, in order to have the benefits of specialized knowledge and focused responsibility, will need to be restricted in its responsibilities—the deeper you wish to see, grip events and control, the more narrowly is it necessary to draw the lines of authority. Consequently, as we have seen, there arises the problem of interrelationship, unification of direction, and the supplemental action of some organization charged with taking the complete comprehensive view. Even in the history of individual nations such emergent problems have yet to be solved, and there the scope of government activity is very wide and highly detailed in each of its particular sections.

At first sight, when we contemplate the duties of the existing and the coming international organizations, it would seem as though an enormous, perhaps impossible, weight were being thrown on the United Nations Organization and especially on its permanent secretariat. Even if the members of the Organization restrict themselves merely to the investigation, the recommendation and the execution of major principles, and do not at all attempt to follow with that mass of detail, which is

78

the very heart and content of national government, their task will be heavy enough. As such it is an unavoidable one. It does not need directly to penetrate into the economies of individual countries, but it must secure the establishment of rules and standards internationally accepted, the implementing of which within the complicated morass of national affairs would necessarily remain with each nation. But, on pain of international collapse, there must be a world-wide interconnecting standard and it must be accepted and acknowledged as a function of international bodies, to apply the standard. Fortunately, we have at our disposal the experience of national governments, the experience of the League of Nations and a developed administrative science to give us guidance and enable progress to come more quickly than it could possibly do without them. What the General Assembly and the Council have to try to inject into International economic and social collaboration is the simultaneous collaboration of the parts as a whole, and collaboration at the very inception of policy: simultaneity and incipiency of action are the twin factors of success in administrative coordination.

EXPERIENCE OF LEAGUE ON COORDINATION PROBLEMS

The League of Nations was faced with this problem of coordination and turned to it on several occasions. Some of its observations are of the highest importance to the present discussion, and the experience of the League in this respect cannot have failed to induce those who established the Dumbarton Oaks Proposals and the Charter to give two chapters to the Economic and Social Council. The Committee for the Coordination of Economic and Financial Questions emphasized that for all its "political severance" the world was daily growing more closely knit, and that this growing interdependence inevitably gave rise to problems that could only be solved by joint effort.[1] Then it emphasized the dynamic element—what

[1] *The Development of International Cooperation in Economic and Social Affairs. Report of Special Committee.* (League of Nations Publication. 1939. General. 3) N. Y., Columbia Univ. Press, Agents, p. 7.

is called the "irresistible dynamism" arising out of economic and social necessity and innovations, and emphasized the fact that it is not possible to clamp down a world inert and motionless. The theme is clearly the need for a continuous organization to observe and to provide for changes that are taking place. On this the Committee, of which Sir Stanley M. Bruce of Australia served as chairman, said: [1]

"The abundance of life cannot be compressed within rigid limitation. There are too many factors of change: members of populations; immigration; revolution in technical processes; constant changes in the balance between the various kinds of agriculture and industrial production, and in the respective roles of machinery and manual work; in the organization of labor; in the transformation of raw materials; in financial and commercial relations; in transport aviation and wireless."

Hence, the Bruce Committee admitted the need for cooperation and insisted upon the need for a mechanism to confront the many changeable progressive interrelationships of the various branches of economic and social effort. The Committee itself was established because it was more and more borne in upon the Members of the League as a result of their constant meetings and discussions that the work and spheres of interest of individual committees of the League, such as the Economic Committee, the Financial Committee, the Fiscal Committee, the Committee of Statistical Experts, the Demographic Committee, the Delegation on Economic Depressions, etc., were vitally interconnected. The Committee itself said: [2]

"It is now being more fully understood how intimately the various problems are interconnected, one with another. Social welfare, the care of the child and the protection of the family link up directly with the problems of better housing and of better feeding. These in turn are in many ways dependent on economic conditions, on transportation facilities and on methods of taxation. . . . Behind and in a sense governing all these great questions is the yet greater question of population—the problem is presented on the one hand

[1] *Ibid.*, p. 8.
[2]. *Ibid.*, p. 15.

by rapidly growing populations in some parts of the world and on the other by the diminishing birth rate in many of the countries and the changing age of their populations."

The Committee admitted that the growing interdependence of economic and social questions had had its reflection in the increasing measure of coordination between the League's committees and a recent concentration and regrouping within the Secretariat which was in the course of being effected.

In the opinion of the Committee, the League rendered the following valuable services to this task of coordinated development:

"The League's resources enable it in the most economical possible way: (a) To collect and sift evidence drawn from all over the world; (b) To obtain the services of the best experts in the world working without reward for the good of the cause; (c) To arrange meetings between experts working in the same fields enabling them to discuss their preoccupations, their success and failure; (d) To provide the essential links between the experts and those responsible for policy; (e) To provide constant and automatic opportunities for statesmen to meet and discuss their policy; (f) To provide thereby means for better understanding of the aims and policies of different nations; (g) To provide machinery for the conclusion of international conventions."

This list of services rendered by the coordinating facilities of the League is the minimum core of the work that should be done under the authority of the Economic and Social Council. But it is the minimum only. In addition to this list, over and above it, there are others for which the Council must in the future be responsible and of which it must, on pain of world economic distress, become the leading and energizing advocate. We shall return to this in a moment.

Before leaving this part of the discussion we draw attention to one other feature of the Report of the Bruce Committee. In order to fulfill its first aim "to increase the efficiency of the work as a whole" it proposed several new measures. They were, apart from publicity which was designed to give additional vigor and efficiency to the work, these:

"(a) To bring all this part of the work of the League under the supervision of an agency which would be both effective and representative; (b) To meet the fact that this development in the nature of the work results in a growing interconnection between the activities of the different organizations, and that, therefore, a coordinating direction is more and more required; and (c) To give states, not Members of the League, the opportunity of the fullest possible cooperation in the work itself as well as in its direction and supervision."

Some comments on the foregoing are essential at this stage. It is hoped that proposal (c) would no longer be an anxiety of the U.N.O. for it is hoped that all peace-loving states will be Members and, therefore, will both as a right and an obligation participate, and not merely cooperate in the economic and social work of the Organization. As the Bruce Committee observed, the effectiveness of international government is a function of cooperation, and of the wish to use the international agencies on the part of the Member States. "Of course, the League is essentially a governmental organization. The constituent members are countries as represented by their governments. Its progress depends upon the effective desire of the governments to use its machinery and upon the possibilities of securing an adjustment of national policies within the spheres in which coordinated and cooperative international action is required, and practical action, to give effect to the work arranged through the League, is in most cases only possible through the executive machinery of national governments."

In order, therefore, to achieve the cooperation which it had demonstrated as necessary, the Committee proposed that the League Assembly should set up "a new organism," to be known as the Central Committee for Economic and Social Questions, to which should be entrusted the direction and the supervision of the work of the League Committees dealing with economic and social questions. This body would be composed (in the first stage) of 24 states, elected by the Assembly, and hereafter the number of states and the term of election would be varied in the light of experience. It was proposed that the Secretary-General of the League should make an annual separate report to the Assembly on the work done in the economic and social fields, in order that this sphere of the League's activities should receive separate and special attention without being overshadowed by debates on foreign policy. Other recommendations were that the Central Committee should appoint the members of various standing technical committees so far as existing international conventions permitted this, and to appoint new committees and modify, where desirable, the existing structure of economic and social organizations.

The Report also suggested that the whole budget relating to the economic and social work should be examined and approved by this widely representative body before submission to the Supervisory Commission and the Assembly. The Central Committee should be entrusted with the direction and supervision of the work of the committees dealing with economic and social questions. This, I think, may be regarded as the embryo of the present proposals. We may pass from a consideration of the origin and purpose to a consideration of future development.

UNIVERSAL MEMBERSHIP AND DOMESTIC COORDINATION

First, it is essential to have a maximum number of countries in the U.N.O., and equality of representation in the Assembly encourages this membership. If there is a necessary interconnection between the economic and social sectors as they stretch over the entire world through and beyond the boundaries of each individual country, so also is there a connection between the parts of each economic sector which lie within the territories of various states, and it is still a truth that the sovereignty and independence of states stand as the formal basis of international relations. Since, according to international law, nations may refuse to become members, and under the accepted interpretation of the Charter, withdraw from membership for cause, the development of the organization in the future may be thus obstructed. It is a simple truism that the first requirement of such an organization is the inclusion and retention of all states.

Now this implies a duty, which if carried out properly, would be the beginning of interconnection between the various individual international economic organizations without even any further machinery. Since each country is a party not only to conventions establishing international agencies like the World Fund, the Food and Agriculture Organization, the International Civil Aviation Organization, the Education and Cultural Organization, the International Labor Organization, etc. but is a member of more than one, and perhaps of all, the first element of coordination of the work of all of them lies in the choice and adequate instruction by each government of its delegates, so that a personal connection between the work of the several agencies might thereby be established. The experience of the past in international organization, and certainly of the domestic government of individual states, shows that it is possible. The delegates to the governing bodies and the international conferences of each international agency may render a considerable service if they possess that breadth of mind which instantly perceives the connection between the policy which its organization must pursue, and the benefits which it may obtain from coordination with the work of other organizations, as also the damage which it might do to itself and to the other organizations by ignoring the functional compulsion to collaboration. This is a task for governments. The nature of that task is implied very clearly in an observation made by Sir Frederick Leggett at the 91st Session of the I.L.O. Governing Body (as Government Representative for Great Britain) when the problem of the relations between the I.L.O. and other international bodies was being debated. In the Minutes his remarks are summarized as follows:[1]

[1] *Minutes of the 91st Session of the Governing Body of the International Labour Office,* cited above, p. 24, par. 5.

"The International Labor Organization did not function *in vacuo,* apart from Governments and other bodies. All the members of the Governing Body were aware of the measures which were being planned in their respective countries in other fields. In Great Britain, the Government was in close consultation with the employers and workers, and the British Government was convinced, for instance, that it could never have mobilized the nation's resources for the war effort as it had done without the help of employers and workers. It should not be thought that the Government representatives on the various bodies set up to deal with food and agriculture, relief and other matters, to which previous speakers had referred, acted on their own behalf without consultation with their Governments, and without any coordination between their instructions and those given to their Governments' representatives on the Governing Body."

It is, therefore, a special task of some agency in the government of each state to try to act as the unifying mind to produce a coherent design in all its interests in the international organization, and to instruct, educate and influence its delegates in the necessity of being alert for and responsive to the need of cooperation. This holds good both of general political delegates as well as economic experts, and it ought even to penetrate through to the Secretariat. Before the beginning of World War II both the French and British Governments had moved toward the formation of a special division of their administration to synthesize the Governments' varying activities in the League of Nations. A very much bigger and more deliberate task now faces the nations. Some thought has been given to this, but not yet enough by a sufficient number of countries.

THE SECURITY COUNCIL AND ECONOMIC AFFAIRS

Secondly, we have already suggested that it would be impossible for the Security Council not to assume responsibilities in the economic and social sphere. At the minimum, it has a concern for sanctions and the relationship of strategic materials to sanctions. Furthermore, it has a responsibility for such preparations and contributions as must be made within the plans of its Military Joint Staff. It is also an important party to trusteeship arrangements and has an official continuing responsibility for the strategic areas. Beyond this, there are other considerations which must compel its continuous attention to economic and social affairs, which, in the Charter are formally attributed to the Assembly. It is responsible for preventing disputes from becoming hostilities. Sometimes those disputes will be disagreements of an economic nature, for example, migration, industrialization, economic competition for markets, exclusive possession of raw materials, access to colonial markets, and so on. "International justice" in the preamble means in part economic fairness and adjustment. It may, therefore, be called upon to consider such possibilities of conflict.

Furthermore, the Security Council has other vital interests in economic and social coordination. It will consist of 11 members, and above all of five members, and even above that, of the Big Three (United States, the U.S.S.R. and the United Kingdom). The eleven, the five and the three must be concerned with two views of power relationships. They will be concerned with the total weight of power, that is (if we exclude strategic geographical position) with economic and social strength, of the eleven, or the five or the three as a whole. And, it can never fail to be a matter of concern to each country composing the eleven, the five and the three what the power relationship is between the members of these collectivities themselves. Such preoccupation will mean that they cannot avoid influencing the general policy within which the Assembly and the Economic and Social Council and the several special international agencies may affect the agriculture, the industry, the balance of population, transit and communications, and tariffs of the whole world. For example, there is a clearly desirable pattern of agricultural production based on a scientific study of diet and of the relative productive capacities of the different countries. If the Food and Agriculture Organization were purely technical, not composed of members of sovereign states with anxieties about security, then the welfare of the world could be immensely increased as each country responded to its recommendations. It might happen that a country hitherto rich in cereals, wheat, corn, barley and oats, might be required to decrease these and produce instead cattle, milk and vegetables. But in the present state of the world, and in its situation for some decades to come, each country would have some reservations regarding its self-sufficiency in war. We may indeed soberly hope for improvements compared with the interwar years, when the countries were running backward into military autarchy. Yet it is manifest that the Security Council would be forced to exercise a qualifying influence over the purely technical considerations of the F.A.O. There would be a strategy of food as well as a policy of abundance. Similarly individual countries and the Security Council would be anxious about the security aspects of tariffs, the location of industry, the advance of international credit and industrialization, and about migration and the rise and fall in the population, etc.

Hence there will always be a marked interest of the Security Council in the policy of the Assembly and the Economic and Social Council and of the specialized international agencies. Either by direct vote and report, or by the indirect process of diplomacy, it will be made clear how far these other bodies, upon whom have devolved either advisory and investigatory or actual executive functions, may go. The Security Council may by the Charter require from each of these bodies directly, or through the Secretary-General, full information and frequent advice so that its burden of responsibility may be properly borne. The other special bodies will independently produce ideas and policies and will have the freedom to carry out their every day responsibilities, yet the Security Council for its part, having the record and the policies before it, will respond with permissions and limits.

The Council of Foreign Ministers of the Five Great Powers, set up by the Potsdam Conference of July 17, 1945, could hardly meet for the various purposes assigned to it—the preparation of the treaties of peace with the defeated countries, the settlement of territorial questions, and the consideration of other questions emanating from the Crimea Conference—without more or less consciously surveying the problems of world economy. Concerned as the several Ministers must be with all the intertwined threads that make up the interest of their own country in the fate of the rest of the world, there is no doubt that they can never in their conversations segregate considerations of power and security from those of world economic welfare, and the claims that each may have to make on the other. Even their preoccupations about the course of their home economies cannot help being expressed in company of the other Ministers. Their minds casually or deliberately would range over all the problems that seemed to them to be international; and of these for many years to come the economic and the social must rank very high. This cannot fail to influence the road taken by the General Assembly, the Economic and Social Council, and the specialized agencies.

Relation to the General Assembly

We now turn to the part of the General Assembly. Its incomparable merit is that it comprises all countries in one great and frequently meeting forum. It is, moreover, given the special responsibility for "international economic and social cooperation," the most convincing sign of which, apart from the vesting Article 60, is its power to elect the 18 members of the Economic and Social Council. Its function should and will be exercised in the following directions. First and foremost, it is the body which, by frequent debate, may affect the mind of the whole by a standard of action recommended in the interests of the whole world. It must search for, discover, elaborate and work for a standard. Its nature has been all too amply discussed. But attention should once more be directed to the fact that until the Charter was drafted, no very definite economic objective had been set forth as the pillar of cloud by

88

day and the pillar of fire by night to guide the Organization. The Dumbarton Oaks Proposals contained none, except the "creation of stability and well-being." But the intervention of the Australian Government resulted in much more specific goals, those of higher standards of living, full employment, and conditions of economic and social progress and development; solutions of international economic, social, health and related problems; and international cultural and educational cooperation; and "universal respect for, and observance of, human rights and fundamental freedoms for all without distinctions as to race, sex, language or religion." While it has not been regarded as part of the purpose of this paper to discuss the clause contained in the quotation marks, it is nevertheless easy to see that some of the fundamental rights and freedoms to which it has reference must in our day be couched in economic terms. It would, for example, be a right to have open access to a job regardless of race, sex, language, or religion where these were not imperative rational disqualifications for the job, technically regarded. The Ukrainian delegate, indeed, offered it as his opinion that "the right to work" was one such right which, though he would not insist, ought to be included. Or, there is the problem of migration, and the discriminations mentioned above.

The detailed policies and practical arrangements necessary to the implementing of these objectives will be the touchstone of its lead to the Economic Council and the Commissions and the Member States.

The mobilization of opinion, and the definition and establishment of international standards, is the really epoch-making function ascribed to the General Assembly by the Charter. Such a function was developed by the League of Nations Assembly in the interwar years. Even if its authority to secure the establishment of conventions were omitted, the value of the I.L.O. as a mere world parliament, where standards are openly debated, would have been more than justification for its existence. Statesmen and experts (it is marvellous but true to affirm) are ashamed to act against the facts as presented in a world forum. They may resist—but they are usually ashamed to do so. The progressive elements in the various countries are, at any rate, encouraged and assisted by the discussions at the international and impartial center.

For one thing, the General Assembly may contribute powerfully to the cooperativeness of states, and to an understanding by the individual governments that they ought to elect their delegates to each of the international bodies so as to promote collaboration. But there is one other point. *The Report of the Committee Appointed to Study the Constitutional Procedure and Practice of the Committees of the League of Nations* [1] drew attention to the indispensable element in the success or failure of the League, namely the degree to which the governments desire to make full use of the League's technical organizations. A note, perhaps of disappointment, can be discerned in the Committee's observation: "Where, however, these conditions do not exist, no possible machinery can do much useful work." But it is preceded by an opinion which may well be reproduced verbatim.

"In the first place, by far the most important condition of effective work by the League's technical organizations is that the governments should desire to make full use of them for assistance in dealing with the problems and the difficulties with which they are confronted. If a given problem is ripe for international action, if the internal policies are sufficiently elastic and capable of modification to make such action possible; and if the governments definitely desire it, real progress will be made. The existing machinery can be effectively used, and where required it can be rapidly adapted."

It would seem to be an obligation of first rank of the General Assembly, and of the Economic and Social Council, to stimulate the desire of the separate governments to make use of the Economic and Social Council and of the several international agencies. They must consider and publicize the

[1] League of Nations Assembly Doc. 16, August 5, 1935, p. 2 (League of Nations Publication 1935. General. 3.) N. Y., Columbia Univ. Press, Agents.

methods by which this might be achieved. But that is not all. It is no special responsibility of any of the individual international organizations itself to consider measures for the coordination of its own work with that of others, or for the establishment of any agency to fulfill functions for which as yet no provision is made, excepting in so far as its own interests were concerned. Moreover, such a body is not likely to be able to press its recommendations forward in the manner or in the quarters which would in practice eventuate in success.

It is the duty of the General Assembly, being above suspicion of an interested party, and with an evident sweep of vision, to survey the whole, continuously developing, field of economic, social and humanitarian activities, and (a) either to make recommendations in detail that an additional agency should be set up or (b) to propose a conference of nations which would prepare an international convention leading to the establishment of a new international agency. This initiative will be especially incumbent upon it in the immediate post-war years. It will no doubt preside at the dismantling of the UNRRA organization; will have to consider whether and when its work is completed; will no doubt be consulted and ought to make recommendations on those great experiments, the Middle East Supply Centre, the Combined Production Boards, etc. Not that it is here suggested that these remarkable international bodies should be retained when their wartime task is finished, but the problem is precisely to have the Assembly deliberate upon the question whether the task is, indeed, finished; and if it should be, whether the assembled secretaries could not be further used in cognate fields.

Again, the function of the General Assembly will be to fulfill a continuous interest in, and supervision of, the Economic and Social Council and of the several agencies. Though it is classed as a "principal organ," the Economic and Social Council acts under the authority of the Assembly. On this subject only this need be said, that the supreme merit of establishing an Economic and Social Council with a continuous responsibility for the coordination of the separate bodies is that it provides an organ analogous to that of Cabinet meetings and Parliaments in individual countries, designed to secure even by their mere presence and the possibilities of debate and open discussion, the harmonious adjustment of the activities of the separate agencies. Where information may be requested, where debates may be instituted, where questions may be pressed, lack of coordination and overlapping and insufficiency of authority for the performance of desirable functions cannot be long-lived, for they are an open challenge. A continuous impression of inefficiency can be registered and there is always the prospect of a recommendation to remedy an unfortunate situation.

The Assembly will exercise a strategic function of lasting and penetrating effect, in the giving or withholding of approval to the agreements between the Economic and Social Council and the specialized agencies which in practice will establish the Council's coordinating authority. What influence this will imply on the Assembly's part will become evident from the analysis of the work of the Economic and Social Council itself.

FUTURE OF THE ECONOMIC AND SOCIAL COUNCIL

We have already [1] enumerated the responsibilities of the Economic and Social Council in relationship to the Assembly above and the specialized agencies below. Its special task is coordination. What form should this take?

This would seem to call for three broad classes of activity: 1. Preparation of general policies for the Assembly to consider; 2. Watchfulness over the activities of the Members and the specialized agencies; and 3. Administrative coordination of the several specialized agencies.

1. *Policies for Consideration of Assembly*

In this field of preparation of general policies, the Economic and Social Council would need to devise some instrument of

[1] Cf. beginning Chap. IV.

regular consultation with the heads of the specialized agencies. At first sight it might be thought that the representative of such special agencies ought to be a delegation of their governing body. If this device were adopted, it might be that the meetings would be too large for effective businesslike debate. At such meetings the specialized agency's Director General, or whatever the title of the administrative chief happens to be, would certainly be present. It would probably be the better arrangement for this administrative chief only to be present at such meetings, in the normal way. He is fully aware of the situation and opinion prevalent in his own organization; and whether he begins his career as an expert or not, years of service make him adequately expert for discussing relationships. Besides this, he is normally accompanied by various necessary attachés, all expert; and he is fully cognizant of the minority and dissenting strains of opinion in his own organization. Thus, there might well be a kind of regular Cabinet meeting of the heads of the special agencies with the Members of the Economic and Social Council, or with a delegation of the Council, or with one or more of its commissions. Such an arrangement is sanctioned by Article 70 which permits the reciprocal participation of the Council, the representatives of the specialized agencies in each other's deliberations. This is an extremely important phase of both collaboration to secure the success of a policy transcending but properly pervading all, and the making of such a policy.

2. *Vigilance over National Policies and International Agencies*

Especially assisted by its Commissions and the appropriate sections of the Secretariat, the Economic Council would be responsible for:[1] the study of the policies pursued by all the governments; analysis of the vicissitudes of economic activity in

[1] League of Nations, *Economic Stability in the Post-War World,* Part II, Report of the Delegation on Economic Depressions, 1945 (League of Nations Publication 1945. II. A. 2.) N. Y., Columbia Univ. Press, Agents, p. 287.

particular countries or throughout the world, disseminating to governments and the public reports of events and suggestions of remedial measures; the calling of consultations between governments, special international agencies and itself; and the recommendation to the General Assembly, to the Members of the Organization and to the special agencies, of world policies to prevent depression and assist economic advancement.

3. *Administrative Coordination of Agencies*

The administrative coordination of the special international agencies requires considered analysis.

First, in no way ought the Economic and Social Council encroach upon the responsibility accorded to the governing bodies, the conferences and secretariats established by the conventions establishing the special organizations. The authority of these bodies must be commensurate with their responsibilities if they are to carry through their work with vigor and zeal. In no way should it be suggested, or thought, that an interference with their everyday responsibilities by the Economic and Social Council is desirable. This is important for the success of the separate agencies, and the successful fulfillment of the functions of the Economic and Social Council. It is desirable that each should be saddled only with the praise and blame for which it is really responsible. It would be unfortunate if, in pursuit of some excessive interpretation of its powers, the Economic and Social Council were to intervene in the daily responsibilities of any one of the special agencies. For this would involve two undesirable consequences. These special agencies have been established by treaties made by a certain number of signatories, and those signatories have devolved some part of their independence and authority to the international body so created. It should be for the signatories, in the first place, to seek to extend or to diminish their authority, and, for them, if necessary, to intervene in the financing and procedures of the special agencies in question. Any inter-

94

vention by the Economic and Social Council would be, therefore, an affront to the signatory states, especially as it would be
a confrontation of a body composed of 18 states with special
agencies supported by 30, 40 and more nations. But what is
just as important as the formal impropriety is the practical
damage done by such interference, the dislocation of the
relationships of confidence between the signatories and their
own special agency's governing body, conference and secretariat. On the other hand, a clear statement of the responsibility of individual agencies is necessary. No special agency
should ever be in a position to ascribe a failure to the Economic
and Social Council, nor to slacken its efforts because it has been
taken for granted that some other authority has the power to
do what it ought to do.

Secondly, therefore, the extent to which the Economic and
Social Council, for the General Assembly, pursues its inquiries
and recommendations into the administrative budgets of the
various agencies would need to be limited. It cannot be limited
by the stipulation of permissible detail, because even an inquiry about the work of a single officer may, at any moment,
raise issues of principle and policy. Such a profundity of investigation should not be excluded, but it should stop at the
point of inquiry and recommendation. It is important in the
highest degree that there should be no suspicion of exercising an influence upon actual appointments from the director
general of the secretariat of the specialized agencies down-
wards to the merest clerical assistant. The responsibility of a
special agency, of its director and all its staff, should be definite and unassailable. There is no harm in the Economic and
Social Council investigating and formulating general principles of appointment, tenure and qualifications for all the
bodies. A time may even come, when, for certain general
classes of international secretariat, it might even sponsor an
Appointments Commission, but for the moment that is beside
the point. The essential principle is that within each organization there shall be freedom of action which implies concentra-

tion of responsibility, i.e., freedom of administrative operation, freedom of spending, freedom of appointment and dismissal.

The subject of finance imposes a peculiar duty on the Economic and Social Council: at once to defend against unreasonable public attack the necessary aggregate expenditures that are demonstrably necessary to each special body, and to persuade those bodies that the total sum spent by each country on international government arouses discontent, however small it is compared with the enormous, but less arithmetical, index of advantage obtained from international cooperation. League of Nations expenditures (including I.L.O. and World Court), which at their highest point in 1932 amounted to the relatively small sum of 6.5 million dollars, were almost everywhere regarded with discontent by opponents of international action, and those ignorant of what the League accomplished. The sum to be spent in the future will be far larger: it must be safeguarded by the Economic and Social Council counselling against extravagances.

In this connection, it seems to me relevant that the twenty years or more which have elapsed since the League settled into its work on the side of its "Technical Organizations" have witnessed a decided movement away from a theory of organization which prevailed at the beginning and the steady transition to a new concept. The Technical Organizations of the League were founded on a principle put forward by one of the ablest innovators in international government, Sir Arthur Salter. The principle was:[1]

"1. Where international work requires the continuous cooperation and executive action of several governments (and the most important work does require them), it is essential that the responsible authorities in the several national administrations should be brought

[1] Salter, Sir James Arthur, *Allied Shipping Control*, N. Y., Oxford Univ. Press, 1921, p. 257 (Carnegie Endowment for International Peace: Economic and Social History of the World War (British Series), Edited by James T. Shotwell).

into direct contact with each other. No external organization can effectively control and coordinate their action.

"2. This direct contact will sometimes take the form of conferences or councils of departmental ministers dealing directly with each other and not through Foreign Offices. These meetings will secure the necessary *authority* for action, but in themselves they will not be sufficient if the work is intricate and consecutive in character, because they will necessarily be brief and irregular.

"3. Contact, and indeed regular contact, must therefore be established between the appropriate permanent officials of the several national administrations. It is important that these officials should (where possible) continue to exercise executive authority in their own departments, and where geographical reasons prevent this, that they should at least be specialists and continue to exercise a decisive influence on them. The officials must enjoy the confidence of the respective Ministers, must keep in constant touch with their policy, must within a considerable range be able to influence their action, and they must have an accurate knowledge of the limits of their own influence.

"4. These officials must work together enough to know each other well, to develop mutual trust and confidence, or at the worst to judge accurately the limits within which they can trust each other. They must in their own national departments represent the international point of view, and in their international organization they must represent the national point of view. It is quite as important that they should continue to understand and to influence their national policies, as that they should learn to understand and be influenced by the international point of view and the policies of other countries. . . ."

Much progress was made by this means, through the technical representatives of the various nationalities and their work in instituting conferences, the establishment of conventions, the acceptance of recommendations, and the influence which they severally exerted on their own governments and the administrative departments by communication from Geneva or on returning home. But it was a limited influence, limited by reason of the small power delegated to the organs of the League by the nations which were its members, and limited because no international action was possible until the Council or the Assembly, especially the former, had given authority

97

to their deliberations and conclusions, or until an international treaty had been made. Even then, the problem of the continuing enforcement of agreements arrived at was never solved: the roundabout processes of diplomacy of a particularly velvet-glove type (there was no hand in it!), as the example of even the strongest of the Organizations, the I.L.O., shows, took too long to achieve too little.

The present new agencies on money, credit for development, food and agriculture, are more direct in their authority and its application than were the organs of the League. The nature of their task necessitates that they should be so, or they would not be able to achieve what is needed for world welfare. The other agencies proposed are of a like nature, in their directness of obligation and the constitution of the organization set up for the management of their purpose. There is rather more force, coherence, authority, and determination about the new agencies than about the congeries of League Technical Organizations. This firmer grip and greater authority of each of the special agencies needs to be well concerted, so as to achieve simultaneously their own resolute action and progress, and the pulling together of them all for the common purpose.

THE INTERNATIONAL SECRETARIAT

Much discussion has in recent years revolved about the establishment and development of an international secretariat.[1] The idea has gained hold in some quarters and is developing, of a great and unified corps of international officials comprising all branches of the various agencies of international activities which would comprise the secretariat of the United Nations Organization itself, that part of it which is to serve the Assembly and its Committees, the Economic and Social Coun-

[1] Cf. Ranshofen-Wertheimer, Egon F. *The International Secretariat: A Great Experiment in International Administration,* Washington, The Carnegie Endowment for International Peace 1945; *The International Secretariat of the Future,* London and N. Y., Royal Institute of International Affairs, 1944.

cil and its committees and commissions, and the secretariats of the special agencies. The number might run up to 3000. The purpose of the suggestion is excellent: to offer a career, a profession, possibly life-long, in the service of international government, with the opportunity of transfer and promotion from one agency to another as occasion affords, and, by an amalgamation of the various special agencies to produce something of the *esprit de corps* that is to be found in some of the best civil services in the world. Such an *esprit de corps* would, by the way, if it existed, act as a deterrent to the separative and demoralizing influences of national pressures and undue nationalism in the officials of international organizations.

Though this is a laudable purpose, warnings must be sounded. First, it would be essential for the General Assembly to take this as one of its continuing topics of discussion and examination; and, in the course of time, it might be able to propose and secure establishment of something like an international civil service commission, though chiefly for the "general" classes like clerical assistants, translators and executive officers, but not for specialists. (If it did, there would eventually be some connections of interest, not service, between such a commission and the International Education Organization which is being established.) But one other thing is observable in the development of government, within nations, in our time. The movement for the unification of the offices of the several departments of government was very strong and properly so 25 years ago but has now reached its highest point, *and is in fact receding*. It is receding, because it is felt that something of the freshness, the initiative and the sting of responsibility is lost in each individual department when it is merely a part of a vaster apparatus. Obviously, this is a matter of proportion and degree. It is one that cannot be solved at this moment and on paper, except by repeating the warnings already given. Of these the principal one is that though part of the machinery of coordination is to be found in the collaboration of agencies and, in the course of time, the advent of a unified, though not altogether single, international secretariat, the greatest care should be taken in every particular that the individual responsibility of the special agencies should not be enfeebled, but on the contrary fostered.

Coordination of the Special Agencies

The next task of the Economic and Social Council flows from the separative nature of the specialized international agencies. It would seem to be a fatality of corporate bodies, whether national, municipal or industrial, that once they have gained a corporate existence and are vested with defined responsibilities, there is nourished in them a conceit of their own powers and an envy of the powers of others. They are prepared to extend their functions and responsibilities if they are allowed to take over completely the functions of a rival body. But in the absence of any external power over them, and with all the good will in the world in the execution of their own responsibilities, they seem to wish to extend their own power but not to permit any other body with cognate authority to enter into their own dignified sphere. In fact, they will interfere with others where it is feasible, and not necessarily from malice or love of authority, but because they believe that their own assigned function demands it. They become introspective, and tend to magnify the importance and value of their own work as compared with that of other organizations. They become exclusive, monopolistic and separative. This holds good, as any firsthand insight into international administration between 1919 and 1945 will show, of the special international agencies. At the least, they are not always likely themselves to think of inviting the cooperation of others who are potentially rival agencies. They need prompting. These thoughts are amply illustrated in the experience of the I.L.O.[1] and the Food and Agriculture Interim Commission in its earliest stage. UNRRA, on the other hand, invited cooperation through ob-

[1] Cf. *Minutes of 91st Session of the Governing Body of the International Labour Office*, cited above, p. 15.

100

servers, and from the outset certainly benefited considerably thereby.

Therefore, some body is required outside of them which will assume the following responsibilities: (1) To survey the powers of each body and discover whether they ought to be increased or decreased, that is, regardless of whether there are other bodies which by reason of their own scope of authority ought to surrender or take over the powers in question; (2) To contrive that where these bodies can help each other they do actually enter into cooperative effort; (3) To avoid expense due to overlapping; (4) To suggest new functions and the organizations appropriate to them; (5) To have under continuous review the activities of all the organizations in relation to developing needs and supreme international economic and social objectives which require common action; and (6) To make recommendations for action where an appropriate international organization does not exist, and where through political reasons it is unlikely to be established.

Now neither the General Assembly nor the Economic and Social Council is provided by the Charter with coercive authority to fulfill the functions allotted to it. They cannot force any special body into cooperation; they can do no more (but it is much) than point to a clear pledge by Member States. Therefore, they may only proceed in one or more of the following ways:

(1) They can convene and persuade an international conference to change the constitution of each criticized agency.

(2) They can exert an influence by debate, by ventilation and by agitation. The officials of international agencies are extremely sensitive to criticism from outside, especially the criticism of external experts and politicians, and particularly those who have an important place in their national public opinions. For these men may at least affect their appropriations by making their criticisms public later on in their own countries, and most of all in their parliaments and cabinets. It would seem at first sight as though the secretariat or the

governing body of the conference of such an agency would harden in its attitude in face of outside criticism. There is in fact some smarting. But the hazards of obstinacy are greater than the hazards of yielding.

(3) The power to stimulate the specialized agencies is increased by the authority given to the Economic and Social Council to obtain reports from the Members of the United Nations Organization directly, regarding the steps they have taken to give effect to the recommendations of the Council and the recommendations of the General Assembly on matters falling within the competence of the Council.

(4) The power is even further enhanced by the authority available to the Economic and Social Council (Article 71) to consult with non-governmental organizations which are concerned with matters within its competence. This opens to the Economic and Social Council all the influence which may be exerted either nationally or internationally by bodies like the International Federation of Trade Unions, the World Trade Union Congress, and the International Chamber of Commerce. Such bodies could be prevailed upon to lend their influence generally in their own countries to affect public opinion; or, they might in appropriate ways, be used to induce a Government to advise its representative on any of the specialized agencies of the policies advocated by them. Arrangements such as those referred to may be freely made by the Economic and Social Council with respect to international organizations, and with national organizations after consultation with the Member of the United Nations concerned. Thus, probably as a result of the experience of the I.L.O. which has been much fortified in its power by the fact that its membership consists not merely of representatives of Governments but of nominees of employers' and employees' organizations, and because the latter has a connection with the vitals of the social and economic life of the respective countries in addition to the usual rather tenuous diplomatic type of connection furnished by the Foreign Office or somebody approved thereby,

the Economic and Social Council has been given a most important opportunity of making such connections, with all that these mean in richness of immediate experience and the power to get things done.[1] On this matter one more thing may be said. It was an ambition of some of the framers of the Covenant of the League of Nations to have sufficient delegates per nation to allow of the representation admitting non-official members to represent bodies of opinion not in the government. The ambition was fulfilled in a few cases; but, on the whole the policy was abortive. The Economic and Social Council now has a similar and clearly indicated opportunity; it can be an extremely valuable one.

The Secretariat of the United Nations Organization will serve the Assembly and the Economic and Social Council and its commissions. That secretariat will be in contact with the secretariats of the special agencies. It will require diplomacy of the highest quality on the part of the supervising secretariat to draw the special agencies into good cooperative relationships with itself, and create in their secretariats such relationships, by sheer reasoning, persuasion, investigations and all those other influences which sometimes constitute a triumph of the purpose of an organization over its mechanism and

[1] The tripartite composition of the I.L.O. has been very useful in that it means a direct representation of social groups, not merely governments, in official international councils. The I.L.O. was anxious not to lose this. Mr. Paul Martin, C. M. P., Parliamentary Assistant to the Canadian Minister of Labor said (Canadian House of Commons) March 20, 1945, "The proposal as outlined today is that by agreement the future relationship of the International Labor Office and the world security organization should be determined with the social and economic council. That is a body wholly made up of governments on which the workers of the world will have no representative at all, and I should think that this would be a serious violation of the tripartite principle of the International Labor Office. The International Labor Office should be given access, not to the social and economic council, but to the assembly of the world security organization. For ultimately, of course, the International Labor Office must be subservient to the world security organization; but let it be subservient to a body that represents the ultimate power of governments and not to a body that has merely delegated power and one on which the workers and employers have no representative."

103

vested interests. I am unable to see that the Commissions could take the place of the Technical Organizations of the League, for these presumably would be replaced at once or later by the special international bodies. But, they would be necessary until the field were fully occupied by the special agencies; and so, between the Economic and Social Council and the nations, there would be the Commissions. And, presumably, there would be a permanent need for intermediate administrative groups to link the occasionally-meeting Economic and Social Council and the various specialized bodies—permanent caretakers for the Council, and advisers to it, and subsequently executants and communicators of its decisions in relation to the agencies. This seems to me to call rather for a Secretariat Committee or groups rather than Committees of technical and national representatives.

(5) The Economic and Social Council would need to devise means of cooperation between the various agencies. First and foremost, comes its status as a body able to make itself the repository of all information. It may proceed in one of two ways, to have all the information required by an agency sent to the Council in the first place, and then itself pass on the information required, thus acting as a clearing-house. This is not desirable, though there is no reason why the information should not be sent to the Secretariat of the Economic and Social Council as a duplicate of that sent to the special agencies. The other way is to lay down rules and regulations which will be embodied in the constitutions of the several agencies stipulating that information required by a special agency be given by those that have it to those who need it.

This is one of the most important functions that the Economic and Social Council can exercise, for it is at the moment of inception of a policy that collaboration can be most fruitful. It has already been suggested that the *ideal* international cooperation would be to have a single mind playing on all the international possibilities, and the purpose of this is the furthest from totalitarian or dictatorial. This is an extreme way of indicating that at the first conception of an idea the elements which might affect its success or failure should come into play immediately, so that a concerted collaborated policy comes into being with a merging of all aspects of the question. It would be the task of the Economic and Social Council to discover the appropriate mechanism and procedure for this. Something like the phrase in the I.L.O. Declaration empowering it to "examine and consider" is required. In the Constitution of the F.A.O. provision is made for agreements between public international organizations with related responsibilities on methods of cooperation.

It would be possible to give to each separate organization the responsibility for asking for such information at any time convenient to it. But there must be a body which has the power to support every legitimate demand of one agency upon another, and such a body would be the Council, continuously served by its officials and commissions. Under the League of Nations' arrangement, the I.L.O. was obliged to give information to the Secretary-General whenever he requested it, and it was able to receive information from him as it needed it. It should be the right of a special agency to appeal to the Economic and Social Council when in pursuance of this right it had asked for information and it had been denied or delayed; and the Council ought to have the right to secure the information for that body. But it must not be believed that mere receipt of information will satisfy the needs of international collaboration. The Netherlands Government's representative on the Governing Body of the I.L.O. gave point to this when he said: [1] "The Office could not confine itself to submitting documents or asking permission to send an observer when questions of life and death for the workers were at stake, and the workers' organizations should be associated in the consideration of such questions from the beginning through tripartite repre-

[1] See *Minutes of 91st Session,* cited above.

105

sentation of the I.L.O." The power of the Council to obtain reports from Member States regarding their effectuation of recommendations is one way to implement the information-circulating responsibility.

(6) The methods of practical cooperation between the specialized agencies are various. For example, the Economic and Social Council might require that wherever the conference or governing body of one agency has upon its agenda a subject which directly or indirectly affects the execution of the responsibilities of any other agency, observers must be invited from the first agency. Or, it might require a change in the constitution of the various special agencies so that joint sessions would be called for in certain defined spheres of action. On the other hand some subjects might be dealt with by joint committees either with the power of settling the matter, or of referring the agreement reached by such a joint committee back for ratification to the agencies. Thus, the International Institute of Agriculture and the I.L.O. cooperated through a Mixed Committee on Agricultural Questions. The Permanent Mandates Commission included the I.L.O. in its membership. It may be felt by some that the mere representation of one agency on another can mean only the force of one vote among many. This is a misapprehension of the power of representation in such international bodies. A mere vote rarely settles an issue in such a forum. There is a strenuous, patient, careful process of both technical and political accommodation until the maximum feasible answer to the problem in the circumstances of the time is reached. In this process, regardless of the smallness of the representation in votes, arguments effectively put and validly founded have their full effect on policy. But it must enter at the beginning.

(7) Finally, the Economic and Social Council will fulfill the responsibility of coordination best if it has the redistribution of the functions of the specialized agencies continuously in mind. It is theoretically feasible so to define and distribute the functions of different international organizations that

they do not overlap and that no gaps are left. If, then, the responsibilities are left to each, and if they carry out their responsibilities, the result is a unification of direction of them all.

REGIONAL CONFERENCES

The Council will encourage or institute regional conferences on economic, social and humanitarian problems. The authority for this does not and need not appear directly in the Charter, for this is a matter of instruments not principles. It is always a little discomforting to suggest regional differentiation in economic, social and humanitarian matters, because it is difficult to define a region, and unpleasant to think that separate areas might pursue competitive or hostile policies. But what is meant is roughly this. Some countries by reason of their proximity and certain common characteristics of geography and climate and location or the chance of history, have some problems in common. For example, China and India have the common problems of great agricultural areas with considerable industrial opportunities but an extremely low standard of living, and both look also to the development of the Pacific. So also, most of the Latin American countries have a number of economic development problems in common. Again, the Middle East has during World War II been economically stimulated as never before, both agriculturally and industrially. These are problems not special to one country nor common to the whole world. They are in and of the world; but, in addition, they are special problems. The word "regional" is not used here, and certainly ought never to be used, in the sense of a unified economic area marked off from the rest of the world and properly pursuing its own self-sufficient interests. The specialization of labor and the distribution of world trade do not follow such a pattern; nor are the lands of a region self-sufficient even when grouped together. Their connections are world-wide and it is important that that world-wide scope should be maintained. But the economists

107

and statesmen of those areas still feel that they can achieve much for the development of their own areas if they meet together, with a proper secretariat of experts available to advise them, if, in short, there is special concentration on the problems of their area. For example, the I.L.O. instituted an Inter-American Committee to Promote Social Security in December 1940. The Conference held at Santiago de Chile from September 10–16, 1942,[1] called to promote the economic security of workers and their families, formulated a continental program and drafted a charter of basic principles, known as the "Declaration of Santiago de Chile." The Committee has a permanent organization, with headquarters at Lima, Peru, to foster an interest in the problems of Central and South America. This does no harm to anyone else, and there is much good because the solidarity itself is a psychological stimulus to interest and hard work for the success of the policies proposed. Similarly, in the International Labor Conference of May 1933, representatives of China and India proposed that a Far Eastern Regional Conference should be called. Another was proposed for the Middle East. No doubt the Economic and Social Council could foster such special regional bodies, and itself might have commissions and committees to consider the welfare of such areas and perhaps draw its recommendations to the attention of the special agencies if they themselves did not independently take action.

NON-SELF-GOVERNING AREAS

The possibilities of regional interest groupings, and therefore of commissions of the Economic and Social Council to pay special attention to them, might well merge into the responsibilities which the General Assembly and the Economic and Social Council shoulder in relation to the Trusteeship

[1] See " 'A New Structure of Social Security.' The Work of the Inter-American Conference on Social Security . . . ," *International Labour Review*, XLVI (December 1942), p. 661–91.

Council of the Organization over non-self-governing areas. To fulfill the principle (Article 73) that the administering authority shall recognize by practice that the interests of the inhabitants of these territories are paramount, and fulfill the sacred trust of promoting to the utmost the well-being of the inhabitants, an interest in the actions of the administering authority will have to be exercised continuously from the outside. In particular, the obligation to ensure the political, economic, social and educational advancement, their just treatment and their protection from abuses contains a large economic and social element which is of the essence of the obligations and functions of the General Assembly and the Economic and Social Council.

The administering authorities have a special obligation to transmit to the Secretary-General statistical and other information of a technical nature relating to economic, social and educational conditions in their territories. This would be indispensable to a judgment of whether the obligations were being fulfilled, and whether the principle of good-neighborliness in a social, economic and commercial sense to the interests and well-being of the rest of the world (Article 74) was more than a word. In these affairs the Economic and Social Council, seised with the promotion of a policy of economic stability and well-being, of raising standards of living and securing full employment, would in any case be an important factor, and a party to them as of right. Its advice on the reports to be called for, and the fitting of the rights and duties of these territories into the whole economic world framework, would be of inestimable value. And especially would this apply to the ensuring of equal treatment in social, economic and commercial matters for all Members of the United Nations and their nationals. It is true that the first obligation regarding the areas in trust is to the General Assembly and under its authority to the Trusteeship Council; but it is precisely here that the scope of the Economic and Social Council valuably intersects the sphere of the latter.

It seems clear beyond a doubt that all the foregoing considerations lead to a regular permanent seat of the international organization. If it is to be a clearing-house of information; if there is to be a gathering place of experts, if there is to be the creation of an international secretariat which would exercise a unifying influence upon all these bodies, if there is to be a continuous impact of the opinion of the Assembly and the Economic and Social Council on all the several agencies, and if there is to be the documentary and other material at hand whereby decisions may be properly generated and executed, then there must be one spot, the center of all these collaborating bodies. The buildings and apparatus, archives and libraries serving them all must be centrally and immediately available; and economies are to be obtained thereby. One of the best known and most effective ways of securing cooperation is permanently to lodge the operating, planning and consultative agencies next door to each other, and, if possible, even to house them in the same building.

*   *   *   *

No century ever came near the twentieth, so abounding in the potentialities of material and moral progress. Mankind holds in its mighty hands a body of natural science and an armory of technologies at once almost divine in splendor and diabolical in threat. And, never before, not forgetting the zenith of Athens, has man's brow been so illumined with the comprehension of his duty to all men, or his mind so perspicuous concerning the social principles and organizations enabling him to pursue his happiness in decency and freedom. Is it enough? Can he meet the challenge of self-mastery, the task of regulating his own will, so that he may make his way securely through the pitfalls charted by knowledge and the

110

moral experience of many centuries that signal warning or encouragement?

International institutions like the General Assembly and the Economic and Social Council may seem to be but prosaic additions to the already existing governmental machinery. They are; and it is fortunate that they are. For they happen to be the freely-created embodiment of a will to self-government, instruments of rational mentality and purpose, to help to make and throw the sharp light of science upon the path that must be travelled, and to demonstrate that the only guarantee of world security and welfare for all is a continuing sense of obligation supported by the unrelaxing and devoted work of all. *"All Members,"* runs Article 56, *"pledge themselves to take joint and separate action in cooperation with the Organization for the achievement of the purposes set forth . . ."* The life of the United Nations Organization, and in particular the Economic and Social Council, is entirely dependent on the fulfillment of this pledge. Without this it is derelict.

BIBLIOGRAPHY

Charter of the United Nations. Report to the President on the Results of the San Francisco Conference, by the Chairman of the United States Delegation the Secretary of State, June 26, 1945, Washington, Department of State Publication 2349, Conference Series 71, 266 p.

Condliffe, John B. *Agenda for a Post-War World.* N. Y., Norton, 1942, 232 p.

—— *The International Economic Outlook.* N. Y., the Committee on International Economic Policy in cooperation with the Carnegie Endowment for International Peace, 1944, 30 p.

—— and Stevenson, A. *The Common Interest in International Economic Organization.* Montreal, International Labour Office, 1944. Studies and Reports Series B, No. 39, 135 p.

Feis, Herbert. *The Sinews of Peace.* N. Y., Harper, 1944, 271 p.

Goodrich, Leland M., and Hambro, Edvard. *The Charter of the United Nations: Commentary and Documents,* Boston, World Peace Foundation, 1946, approx. 300 p.

Greaves, H. R. G. *The League Committees and World Order.* London, 1931.

Hansen, Alvin H. *America's Role in World Economy.* N. Y., Norton, 1945, 197 p.

Hearings before the Ways and Means Committee of the House of Representatives on H. J. Res. 111 (Extension of Reciprocal Trade Agreements Act), 78th Cong., 1st sess., April 1943. Testimony of Francis B. Sayre, p. 145–304.

League of Nations. *Commercial Policy in the Post-War World.* Geneva, League of Nations Publication. 1945. II. A. 7. (Agents, Columbia Univ. Press, N. Y. C.)

——. *The Development of International Cooperation in Economic and Social Affairs. Report of Special Committee* (Bruce Committee). Geneva, League of Nations Publication. 1939. General. 3. (Agents, Columbia Univ. Press, N. Y. C.)

113

Mitrany, David. *A Working Peace System; An Argument for the Functional Development of International Organization.* London, The Royal Institute of International Affairs; New York, Toronto, Oxford Univ. Press. Post-War Problems, June 1943, 56 p.

Ranshofen-Wertheimer, Egon F. *The International Secretariat. A Great Experiment in International Administration.* Washington, D. C., Carnegie Endowment for International Peace, 1945, 500 p.

Staley, Eugene. *World Economy in Transition; Technology* vs. *Politics, Laissez Faire* vs. *Planning, Power* vs. *Welfare.* N. Y., Council on Foreign Relations, 1939, 340 p.

United Nations in the Making: Basic Documents, Boston, World Peace Foundation, 1945, 130 p.

APPENDIX

CHARTER OF THE UNITED NATIONS TOGETHER WITH THE STATUTE OF THE INTERNATIONAL COURT OF JUSTICE,

SIGNED AT THE
UNITED NATIONS CONFERENCE ON INTERNATIONAL ORGANIZA-
TION, SAN FRANCISCO, CALIFORNIA, JUNE 26, 1945[1]

(Excerpts)

. . . .

CHAPTER I

Purposes and Principles

Article 1

The Purposes of the United Nations are:

1. To maintain international peace and security, and to that end: to take effective collective measures for the prevention and removal of threats to the peace, and for the suppression of acts of aggression or other breaches of the peace, and to bring about by peaceful means, and in conformity with the principles of justice and international law, adjustment or settlement of international disputes or situations which might lead to a breach of the peace;

2. To develop friendly relations among nations based on respect for the principle of equal rights and self-determination of peoples, and to take other appropriate measures to strengthen universal peace;

3. To achieve international cooperation in solving international problems of an economic, social, cultural, or humanitarian character, and in promoting and encouraging respect for human rights and for fundamental freedoms for all without distinction as to race, sex, language, or religion; and

4. To be a center for harmonizing the actions of nations in the attainment of these common ends.

[1] Department of State Publication 2353, Conference Series 74.

Article 2

· · · · · · · ·

7. Nothing contained in the present Charter shall authorize the United Nations to intervene in matters which are essentially within the domestic jurisdiction of any state or shall require the Members to submit such matters to settlement under the present Charter; but this principle shall not prejudice the application of enforcement measures under Chapter VII.

CHAPTER IV

The General Assembly

COMPOSITION

· · · · · · · ·

FUNCTIONS AND POWERS

Article 10

The General Assembly may discuss any questions or any matters within the scope of the present Charter or relating to the powers and functions of any organs provided for in the present Charter, and, except as provided in Article 12, may make recommendations to the Members of the United Nations or to the Security Council or to both on any such questions or matters.

Article 13

1. The General Assembly shall initiate studies and make recommendations for the purpose of:

a. promoting international cooperation in the political field and encouraging the progressive development of international law and its codification;

b. promoting international cooperation in the economic, social, cultural, educational, and health fields, and assisting in the realization of human rights and fundamental freedoms for all without distinction as to race, sex, language, or religion.

2. The further responsibilities, functions, and powers of the General Assembly with respect to matters mentioned in paragraph 1 (b) above are set forth in Chapters IX and X.

Article 17

1. The General Assembly shall consider and approve the budget of the Organization.

116

2. The expenses of the Organization shall be borne by the Members as apportioned by the General Assembly.

3. The General Assembly shall consider and approve any financial and budgetary arrangements with specialized agencies referred to in Article 57 and shall examine the administrative budgets of such specialized agencies with a view to making recommendations to the agencies concerned.

CHAPTER IX

International Economic and Social Cooperation

Article 55

With a view to the creation of conditions of stability and well-being which are necessary for peaceful and friendly relations among nations based on respect for the principle of equal rights and self-determination of peoples, the United Nations shall promote:

a. higher standards of living, full employment, and conditions of economic and social progress and development;

b. solutions of international economic, social, health, and related problems; and international cultural and educational cooperation; and

c. universal respect for, and observance of, human rights and fundamental freedoms for all without distinction as to race, sex, language, or religion.

Article 56

All Members pledge themselves to take joint and separate action in cooperation with the Organization for the achievement of the purposes set forth in Article 55.

Article 57

1. The various specialized agencies, established by intergovernmental agreement and having wide international responsibilities, as defined in their basic instruments, in economic, social, cultural, educational, health, and related fields, shall be brought into relationship with the United Nations in accordance with the provisions of Article 63.

2. Such agencies thus brought into relationship with the United Nations are hereinafter referred to as specialized agencies.

Article 58

The Organization shall make recommendations for the coordination of the policies and activities of the specialized agencies.

Article 59

The Organization shall, where appropriate, initiate negotiations among the states concerned for the creation of any new specialized agencies required for the accomplishment of the purposes set forth in Article 55.

Article 60

Responsibility for the discharge of the functions of the Organization set forth in this Chapter shall be vested in the General Assembly and, under the authority of the General Assembly, in the Economic and Social Council, which shall have for this purpose the powers set forth in Chapter X.

CHAPTER X

The Economic and Social Council

COMPOSITION

Article 61

1. The Economic and Social Council shall consist of eighteen Members of the United Nations elected by the General Assembly.

2. Subject to the provisions of paragraph 3, six members of the Economic and Social Council shall be elected each year for a term of three years. A retiring member shall be eligible for immediate re-election.

3. At the first election, eighteen members of the Economic and Social Council shall be chosen. The term of office of six members so chosen shall expire at the end of one year, and of six other members at the end of two years, in accordance with arrangements made by the General Assembly.

4. Each member of the Economic and Social Council shall have one representative.

FUNCTIONS AND POWERS

Article 62

1. The Economic and Social Council may make or initiate studies and reports with respect to international economic, social, cultural, educational, health, and related matters and may make recommendations with respect to any such matters to the General Assembly, to the Members of the United Nations, and to the specialized agencies concerned.

2. It may make recommendations for the purpose of promoting respect for, and observance of, human rights and fundamental freedoms for all.

3. It may prepare draft conventions for submission to the General Assembly, with respect to matters falling within its competence.

4. It may call, in accordance with the rules prescribed by the United Nations, international conferences on matters falling within its competence.

Article 63

1. The Economic and Social Council may enter into agreements with any of the agencies referred to in Article 57, defining the terms on which the agency concerned shall be brought into relationship with the United Nations. Such agreements shall be subject to approval by the General Assembly.

2. It may coordinate the activities of the specialized agencies through consultation with and recommendations to such agencies and through recommendations to the General Assembly and to the Members of the United Nations.

Article 64

1. The Economic and Social Council may take appropriate steps to obtain regular reports from the specialized agencies. It may make arrangements with the Members of the United Nations and with the specialized agencies to obtain reports on the steps taken to give effect to its own recommendations and to recommendations on matters falling within its competence made by the General Assembly.

2. It may communicate its observations on these reports to the General Assembly.

Article 65

The Economic and Social Council may furnish information to the Security Council and shall assist the Security Council upon its request.

Article 66

1. The Economic and Social Council shall perform such functions as fall within its competence in connection with the carrying out of the recommendations of the General Assembly.

2. It may, with the approval of the General Assembly, perform services at the request of Members of the United Nations and at the request of specialized agencies.

3. It shall perform such other functions as are specified elsewhere in the present Charter or as may be assigned to it by the General Assembly.

VOTING

Article 67

1. Each member of the Economic and Social Council shall have one vote.

2. Decisions of the Economic and Social Council shall be made by a majority of the members present and voting.

119

PROCEDURE

Article 68

The Economic and Social Council shall set up commissions in economic and social fields and for the promotion of human rights, and such other commissions as may be required for the performance of its functions.

Article 69

The Economic and Social Council shall invite any Member of the United Nations to participate, without vote, in its deliberations on any matter of particular concern to that Member.

Article 70

The Economic and Social Council may make arrangements for representatives of the specialized agencies to participate, without vote, in its deliberations and in those of the commissions established by it, and for its representatives to participate in the deliberations of the specialized agencies.

Article 71

The Economic and Social Council may make suitable arrangements for consultation with non-governmental organizations which are concerned with matters within its competence. Such arrangements may be made with international organizations and, where appropriate, with national organizations after consultation with the Member of the United Nations concerned.

Article 72

1. The Economic and Social Council shall adopt its own rules of procedure, including the method of selecting its President.
2. The Economic and Social Council shall meet as required in accordanec with its rules, which shall include provision for the convening of meetings on the request of a majority of its members.

CHAPTER XIII

The Trusteeship Council

PROCEDURE

· · · · · · ·

Article 91

The Trusteeship Council shall, when appropriate, avail itself of the assistance of the Economic and Social Council and of the specialized agencies in regard to matters with which they are respectively concerned.

120

CHAPTER XV

The Secretariat

. . . .

Article 98

The Secretary-General shall act in that capacity in all meetings of the General Assembly, of the Security Council, of the Economic and Social Council, and of the Trusteeship Council, and shall perform such other functions as are entrusted to him by these organs. The Secretary-General shall make an annual report to the General Assembly on the work of the Organization.

Article 101

1. The staff shall be appointed by the Secretary-General under regulations established by the General Assembly.

2. Appropriate staffs shall be permanently assigned to the Economic and Social Council, the Trusteeship Council, and, as required, to other organs of the United Nations. These staffs shall form a part of the Secretariat.

3. The paramount consideration in the employment of the staff and in the determination of the conditions of service shall be the necessity of securing the highest standards of efficiency, competence, and integrity. Due regard shall be paid to the importance of recruiting the staff on as wide a geographical basis as possible.

CHAPTER XVI

Miscellaneous Provisions

Article 102

1. Every treaty and every international agreement entered into by any Member of the United Nations after the present Charter comes into force shall as soon as possible be registered with the Secretariat and published by it.

2. No party to any such treaty or international agreement which has not been registered in accordance with the provisions of paragraph 1 of this Article may invoke that treaty or agreement before any organ of the United Nations.

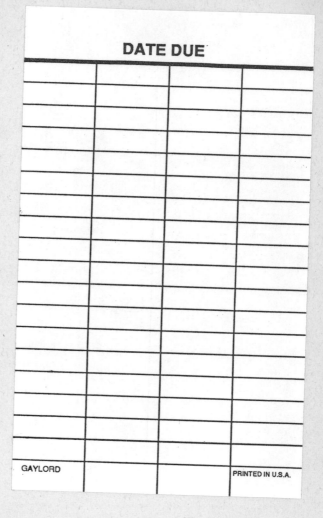

DATE DUE

GAYLORD			PRINTED IN U.S.A.